Karmic Relationships

Karmic Relationships
Healing Invisible Wounds

CHARLES L. RICHARDS, Ph.D.

JODERE
GROUP
San Diego, California

JODERE
GROUP

PUBLISHED BY JODERE GROUP, INC.
P.O. BOX 910147 • SAN DIEGO • CA • 92191-0147 • USA
(800) 569-1002 • www.jodere.com

Book design by CHARLES MCSTRAVICK
Editorial supervision by CHAD EDWARDS

CIP data available from the Library of Congress

ISBN 1-58872-019-5

04 03 02   4 3 2 1
First printing, September 2002

Printed in the United States of America

This book is dedicated
to my parents,
Lydia H. Lockman and Lewis Richards

Your love and support
on this journey
has always been there

contents

part one
The Dynamics of Karmic Relationships

part two
Recognizing Your Invisible Relationship Wounds

Relationships. We are fascinated by them and frustrated by them. We are strangely and intensely drawn to them and at the same time we live in fear of them. They trigger in us emotions that range from love to hate, infatuation to disillusion, from bliss to obsession. But what is most amazing about the people in our lives with whom we are karmicly connected is the depth of emotion and inquiry their presence stirs within us.

What is the inexplicable force behind the magnetic attraction and repulsion we feel while in the throws of a karmic relationship? Why is it that some people push all our buttons and shake us to our core while others leave us unaffected or even disinterested? Why are we drawn time and time again to people and events that stir in us the same longings, or that open within us the same unhealed wounds?

These are some of the mysteries of karmic relationships that my friend Charles Richards explores in this book. His powerful work is an invitation to look beneath the surface of our relationships, to uncover the invisible wounds that keep us repeating the same patterns in our lives and relationships. It is an opportunity to take full responsibility for ourselves and to shatter any illusion we may hold that we are victims of circumstance.

There are many realities. Those that we see, those that others see and those which none of us can see. There is nothing more powerful than bringing our awareness and opening our minds to the forces that can't be seen. Until we do this, the wounds hidden deep in our psyches will continue to draw people, events, circumstances that mirror back to us our lowest, most unconscious selves. The question all of us must ask ourselves is this: Will we choose to stumble through life, slaves to our unconscious, unexamined reactions, or will we look deeper to the place where we know ourselves as the cause of every desirable and undesirable effect?

Reading *Karmic Relationships* offers us the glorious opportunity to understand the spiritual significance of our relationships. Penetrating these unseen forces allows us to take back our power and see our lives through the eyes of our soul.

Debbie Ford
Author, *The Secret of the Shadow*

acknowledgments

Over the years, the people who have inspired me to write and contributed to the realization of this book are numerous. Much love and gratitude to you all for your ongoing inspiration and support.

A deep acknowledgment goes to all my clients for their understanding and willingness to allow the use of their stories to teach and hopefully enlighten those who read this book.

A heartfelt thanks to my friends and agents, Arielle Ford and her soul mate Brian Hilliard, my brother in spirit. Additional thanks to my friend Debbie Ford for prodding me along and illuminating the way, and the entire Ford family for their continued love, inspiration, and support.

Special thanks to Debbie Luican, for giving this book a home and being much more than my publisher; Mark Misiano and the entire staff of the Jodere Group; and my Jodere Group editor, Chad Edwards.

Thanks to my friend Doc Childre for his wisdom, advice, and deep-hearted insight. Also a special thanks to Deborah Rozman and all those at the Institute of HeartMath for their unconditional love and support.

Thanks to Dr. Morris Neatherton for helping to initiate a deeper understanding of past lives and karmic dynamics.

A heartfelt appreciation goes to Deepak and Rita Chopra for their caring and gentle acknowledgment and insight.

To my friend, Jill "Baby G" Mangino, for her loving presence, constant support, and valuable feedback from day one.

To Matthew and Deborah Mitchell, who have always been as close as my heart never wavering in their support and encouragement.

To my tireless friend and editor, Linda Anderson, goes my eternal thanks. She kept me moving forward and always held and nurtured the vision of this book with her ability to organize and structure my message. Her insight was invaluable.

Much appreciation to Harold and Jennifer Ware, both were instrumental at a crucial time with their creative support and suggestions.

To my friends, Ann and Alden Butcher, who were there in the beginning to facilitate and inspire me to be a greater channel to serve others with my message.

To my brothers from other mothers: Tye Smith, Thomas Drayton, Tunde Baiyewu, Vandorn Hinnant, Ian Gardner, Howie Ross, and Conrad Spainhower for the love and support we've shared throughout this journey and beyond.

To all my many friends in the light and sound of spirit who are too numerous to mention for their years of support and encouragement in bringing this book to the public.

To the thousands who've attended my workshops, talks, and classes for the interest, inspiration, and insight they have shared with me over the years.

To Peter and Sherry Skelskey for their encouragement and continuing support of my work.

And finally, words could never convey my heartfelt thanks to Wah Z and the Vairagi, who gave me the gift of guidance and recognition from before the beginning. You have always understood and continue to inspire my highest vision as Soul. Thanks for always being here.

introduction

THE JOURNEY YOU ARE ABOUT TO UNDERTAKE READING THIS BOOK IS ONLY a small mirror of the fascinating one I've had over the years as a therapist. I've covered a vast waterfront of experiences that have been exciting, enlightening, and by the very nature of the work, carries a somewhat spiritual dimension. When you've guided thousands through the death experience and seen through their eyes as they recount what it's like to die, leave the body, and ascend into the life after death, it transforms your understanding profoundly. In my view, all experiences are spiritual whether considered good, bad, painful, elevating, or depressing. They all help us to move to the next step in our quest for spiritual freedom. Whether conscious of it or not, that's what we're all seeking as soul.

I came to this realization when I was about 20 years old after having my first profound conscious journey to the *other side*. It started one afternoon while alone in my father's apartment. I decided to lie down and try an exercise I had learned through my spiritual studies. After a brief lull, I shot quickly into a realm of inner heavenly light and sound in full consciousness. It's impossible to completely describe the realm I witnessed. I found myself in what looked like a magical landscape, enveloped by what appeared to be a physical body composed of subtly shimmering light. The music there was the heavenly sound of flutes, which swirled around and through me as if every atom vibrated with this music. The clouds above glided by and were painted with the colors of the rainbow, but much more vivid. These colors were so vibrant and pure that they seemed alive. And no, I've never had a drug induced psychedelic or hallucinogenic experience. During this whole event, I was more conscious and alert than I'd ever been in my life.

It was intense but blissful, and much more real than anything I'd ever experienced in my earthly body. I was amazed and in awe as I examined my right hand and arm of light along with the surroundings. Everything around me literally danced with energy. This was beyond anything I'd ever imagined. After a while, I decided it was time to return to the body lying quietly on the sofa. When I imagined returning to my physical body, I felt myself dropping as if through different layers of space and time. In seconds, I was back and opened my eyes. I could hear the flute sounds fading in the distance and the bright colors receding as I scanned the walls in the apartment. Once I was completely back, I realized I'd caught a glimpse of what must be heaven. It left me with a knowingness beyond just a belief that such realms existed. It was spiritual, religious, ecstatic, and profound all at once. I also knew that I wanted more. This was my first glimpse behind the *curtain of appearances*. Once having an occurrence such as that, I could only hope that everyone would one day have similar realizations. No doubt it could change the world.

My first glimpse of other worldly bliss gave me an unshakable understanding that there are many levels of existence, and that it's possible to observe them even while we're still in a physical body. A Near Death Experience (NDE) is not necessary. When you've personally had such experiences, all the logical explanations from scientists, skeptics, and others, about abnormal brain chemistry and the like being the cause, are simply amusing. It's as overreaching as the onetime belief that the world was flat, or that the earth was the center of the solar system.

It was during that first Soul Journey that I gained the knowledge that the soul is our true identity and exists separate from the physical body. And, through personal and client experiences, I have been shown that one doesn't *have* a soul—you *are* a soul that has a body. I've had many other spiritual experiences and continue to explore the realms beyond this reality.

Our physical bodies fall away from one lifetime to the next. We, as soul, live on as the very consciousness we recognize as ourselves, and not some spiritual abstraction. It's like purchasing and driving a new car. One day after years of wear, the car gets old, and we eventually need another new car that's more suitable to our current needs.

Writing this book is no doubt part of my life dharma, or higher purpose. The reason I say this is because for years I discounted the call to write it. Yet, the impulse to get this out always remained. For a time, I even distracted myself by training Fortune 500 executives in one of the top training organizations in the country. Still, writing the book, developing and facilitating Soul Journeys therapy stayed with me. Certainly other good books have been written about past lives, karma, and a few about between-lives, but certain key principles were always left out. One, among them, is a realization I've come to as an outcome of my work: *there are no innocent victims regardless of appearances.* Everything that happens to us is the result of our own thoughts and actions, either in this life or a previous one. To truly understand and accept this is profoundly sobering, but also liberating. One thing it does is to eliminate any cause for projecting blame.

I cover a lot of ground in this book by opening a window into the experiences of myself, and the many who've come through my office doors in the years I've been in practice. There have been many times I've wished the world could sit with me and witness the amazing experiences and transformations I've seen. Many of them would challenge the imagination and amaze the observer by going far beyond the parameters of traditional teachings on life, death, and the beyond.

Since I'm a psychotherapist, people most often come to me when experiencing some emotional or physical pain that results from undesirable conditions. The experiences in this book point mainly to those difficult and painful challenges in life and relationships that are quite often rooted in one's karma.

You will read about cases of past-lives and prenatal experiences that at times were tragic, leading to painful trauma and loss resulting in various expressions of fear. Fear, pain, and trauma leave reactive patterns that cause us problems. The past-lives connection to pain or trauma, can lead to the challenges and problems we are facing in our relationships now. Lives lived in relative ease, and without incident or extreme emotional pain, leave no scars. Certainly, we have lived many such lives without the drama of trauma. These past lives don't leave a painful residue, and so seldom are reviewed in my work with clients.

Unlike the familiar stories about people claiming to have been great or well known historical figures such as Napoleon or Cleopatra in their past lives, I've not found this to be true with my clients. When it really comes down to it, most of us were relatively unknown in the historical sense. Nearly all of the thousands of past lives I've seen have confirmed this.

In the pages that follow, I have strategically chosen certain stories from those who have come to me. I believe these stories will illustrate how Karmic Relationships are played out and give examples of the effect their dynamics can have in present lifetimes. I suspect that you will come to some realizations about the hidden dynamics and invisible wounds influencing your own relationships.

Once you have a better understanding of the facets of Karmic Relationships, I will then give you some exercises for your own exploration. It is my hope that you will start to understand the forces that have brought you together with those whom you love or those you do not. And to uncover your deep karmic roots from past-lives, prenatal experiences, or agreements you've made in the between-lives heavenly state. With new recognitions and understandings, you can begin to make the best of all your relationships instead of being under the unconscious influence of *Karmic Wounds* that inhibit your freedom and joy.

My intention of this book is that it be experiential on two levels. First through the stories, and secondly through the exercises presented throughout. It is my desire that you are ultimately guided to your own experience of discovery.

Happy reading.

Charles Richards

part 1

the dynamics of
karmic relationships

chapter 1

Karmic Groundwork

understanding karma

I RECALL, AT FIVE YEARS OLD, LOOKING IN A FULL-SIZED MIRROR AT MY grandparents' home and being surprised by the realization that I had brown skin *in this lifetime.* It somehow seemed different from what I was used to, but when? I recall wondering how or if this would affect my life experience. It was a brief instant of recognition, clarity, and examination of myself. Then as quickly as this awareness surfaced, it subsided and I resumed playing as children do.

Without karma you and I would not be here on this planet. What this means is that the law of cause and effect, or *karma*, is a universal spiritual law and not just a law of physics. This law governs the actions and reactions of all life and all life forms. Karma is basically energy at vibrational frequencies much higher and subtler than we've developed the means to measure. Our karmic mission is one of love, service, and continued spiritual unfoldment here on earth. When we fully understand and apply this law in a constructive, rather than a destructive manner, our karmic lessons here are finished. Living life in a physical body here on Earth is such an opportunity for growth that souls are literally clamoring for the privilege. This is witnessed by the great increase in the world population over the centuries. It makes some wonder where did all these "new" souls come from. When asked this, I try to explain that our earth is not unlike a little anthill on a vacant lot that is surrounded by countless realms of souls (ants) teaming with activity. The influx of additional souls is just a trickle compared to the vastness of what we can't see or understand while trapped in these human bodies.

Over the years, I've grown to understand the ways of karma and the soul by continuing my own personal spiritual explorations. Whenever you experience pain or trauma at the moment of death, or any other time in your life, you go into a relative degree of trance. If it's trauma in the physical body, your attention narrows and fixates on the pain. This fixation of attention causes a trance-like state, which protects your conscious self from overloading. This is why extreme pain or loss can cause you to lose consciousness by passing out. The soul literally passes out of the body as the conscious mind shuts down to prevent a meltdown of the nervous system.

Even though you've consciously shut down to a trance-like state, your unconscious self continues to record all that is happening to and around you with full sensory input of sight, sound, taste, smell, and sensation fully uncensored. Even a light trance, which occurs with minor pain or loss, opens the psyche to uncensored emotional imprints. These imprints take the form of whatever you think or say or what is said to you during pain or loss.

When you regain full consciousness or feel relief, traumatic imprints in the psyche remain with you, locked into the subconscious. The unconscious mind doesn't consider the context of these imprints, but stores them literally with all their raw sensory and emotional input.

As an example, if a woman is sexually assaulted and her attacker tells her she deserves, wants, or has invited the attack, she may have self-doubt and conflict about the experience afterward. Raw emotion mixed with pain shuts down her conscious mind and suggestions pour unfiltered into her subconscious.

If during the assault, the raped woman thought she was being soiled for life and will be undesirable as a mate, her unconscious mind accepts this conclusion literally. The woman's thoughts or the words of her attacker while going through the trauma will later act as post-hypnotic suggestions in her future sexual encounters. Panic and fear cause what she thinks during the rape to directly imprint on her unconscious. This unconscious effect continues even if the woman, after the trauma, reasons that she's still desirable. From an objective viewpoint, this effect seems irrational.

In fatal past-life trauma, full consciousness isn't regained until after the moment of death, when the soul is freed from the painful experience. For this reason the trauma carries over to be dealt with in our next life in a physical body.

Because of this, I found the most effective way to resolve trauma whether in this life, or a past life, is for clients to review the experience in full consciousness without hypnosis. Otherwise, we find ourselves attempting to use a trance state to resolve a trance state. This is not only less effective; it can also result in unintended contamination by the therapist's use of suggestion during a trance.

In this book I've included case experiences that make this understanding abundantly clear. The karma that unfolds in our lives now is shaped by past lifetimes where many of our Karmic Relationships began. The influences during your birth and even the period before birth (prenatal), while still in the womb, can also have a great impact on your personality and karmic destiny. Some of these influences work to your advantage and others to your disadvantage. Dr. Thomas Verney documents much of this in his book, *The Secret Life of the Unborn Child.* If your parents had a difficult marriage, full of conflict and emotional upheavals, this gets recorded by the fetus through the mother's sensory nervous system. As we mature these prenatal episodes act like preinstalled software in a computer. They unconsciously condition our feelings, reactions, and thoughts, and require constant effort to override them even if we somehow become aware of their influence.

The potential advantage to this pre-programming during the prenatal period is obvious if this was a time of comfort, love, and joy for our parents. Additionally if your parents had special skills and talents that were creative/artistic, athletic, scientific, etc., that engaged them during the pregnancy, these also leave an imprint that can work to your advantage as you mature. The most important factor, no matter what your parents went through during this period, is how they handled it and their love for the developing fetus. If they met challenges without denial or repression and faced them successfully, this pattern, or *Gestalt,* is also transferred in the womb and carries forward for you into adulthood. For the most part, we are all born with some handicaps of negative conditioning. This is also a form of karma, which is sometimes referred to as one's fate.

yes, there is good karma

Many people don't realize that karma is not all bad. Much of our karma is also good and desirable, but we most often notice the undesirable or painful events as karma. Any good fortune and success certainly requires hard work to bear fruit but it also requires "good" karma. Sometimes we say the stars are in our favor, or not. Any top Olympic athlete knows that on a given day they may be the absolute best in the world, or just one of the few top performers. When all is said and done the winner is not merely the hardest working, best trained, or most talented, but the one among the best who just happens to be in or get in the "zone" that day when it counts most. Your ability to get in the zone at the crucial time is determined by preparation and the graces of your good karma. Some of us might just call this good luck or bad luck, but understanding karma, you realize there is no such thing as luck. How often do you take the time to be thankful for the good that comes to you? This is karma too, and those incidents and days when lady luck seems to be smiling down upon us are also the result of our self-created karmic conditions. To recognize and acknowledge them is an expression of unconditional love. Such recognition reinforces the good that comes to us.

I've learned, and it must always be remembered, that desirable karma results from the good that you do even in small ways. You move beyond karma when you do the right thing without concern for the karma it may bring. Actions such as these are the result of that very familiar four-letter word called *love*. Unconditional love will eventually liberate us from "negative" karma.

Actually, karma itself, is impersonal and beyond good and bad. These are human labels and judgments. Karma is just the energetic expression of cause and effect that governs the actions of all life. We label it good or bad depending on whether it makes us happy or sad, or brings us pleasure or pain. It's all a matter of interpretation, and even painful karma has its value in the refinement of soul. Karma simply means that what you do, or did, comes back to you in full and in kind.

For the caterpillar trapped in the cocoon, the struggle to emerge is no doubt painful. If that caterpillar could speak it might say that this is a miserable circumstance, being stuck in this cocoon. It's a very bad karma. But once it escapes the restriction of the cocoon and is transformed into a beautiful butterfly, the pain and struggle is quickly forgotten. It faces a new life as it wings its way to freedom into a bright new world drawn naturally to the beauty of nature.

between-lives

As part of taking this "karmic journey" with you, I've also included the period between-lives. In some ways, this is the most profound part of my work. The reason for this is that between lifetimes the soul has a much greater awareness of itself as a spiritual Being beyond the limitations of a physical body. Here, soul is home and feels at home. Upon first entering this realm, one client of mine burst into tears of joy and proclaimed that she was finally home again. This is where you meet with loved ones and your Soul Group, review past lives, see the source and nature of Karmic Relationships, receive specialized training, or learn higher spiritual truths. Then comes the task of selecting your next lifetime and preparing for your sojourn into another physical body. This choice is based on numerous karmic factors spanning many previous lifetimes, Karmic Relationships, expressions of love and interest.

Let's use a car once again as a metaphor. If you've ever shopped for a new car, and most of us have, you may have some idea of what it's like to choose a new incarnation. The make and dealership would be like the family and parents you choose. The model of car could reflect your appearance, health and physical integrity at birth. It could also include your primary activity in that lifetime requiring beauty, power, intelligence, mere dependability, or a combination. The standard features are based on your previous karmic qualifications from past lives and might reflect intelligence, race, gender, country of birth, handicaps, special skills, and abilities. Extra options might reflect the accumulated good karma from previous lifetimes you are willing to spend on things, such as better health, advanced education, better cognition, special skills, loving parents, etc. The time of your new incarnation would be tied to many factors involving the availability of the conditions you want and the other souls you wish to incarnate within the coming lifetime.

Once all these parameters have been determined, there will be certain physical incarnations that will meet most or all of what you are looking for. Among these options, you must choose one. Most likely your choice will involve some compromise, as all on your list may not be available exactly when and where you want to be reincarnated. You will have wise and familiar guides and advisors to assist you in this process of selection.

Your effectiveness in your new lifetime can then be greatly enhanced in the *between-life* state by spending time studying and preparing for how to make best use of the time while in your new incarnation. I'd call this rehearsing your ideal dharma or life destiny. Like buying a new car, some souls accept the options readily available to them and just choose one. Others plan, study, research, consult, and negotiate their options within predefined limits. This example is at best an approximation of how the process unfolds on the other side.

This is a spiritually rich period full of freedom and possibilities for many souls. Even for souls who've hurt and abused others, it's a chance to prepare for another round with the opportunity to atone for past mistakes or poor choices.

the evolution of soul journeys therapy

Years ago, I had little choice but to eventually take my therapeutic work in this direction because the results spoke for themselves. With a love of people, psychology, and personal growth, my search has been to find the most effective way to help those who come to me resolve their life challenges and relationship conflicts. Traditional theories of psychology and methods of therapy all had value for me, and I have studied and used many of them along the way.

In the beginning of my practice, my personal preference was for the Jungian model. I valued the richness of insight and understanding this form of therapy gave me in working with my clients. However, the symbolic metaphors and interpretations still felt one step removed from the reality of what people on the street had to face in their every day lives. Furthermore, it often took months or years to get any noticeable results. From my earlier studies of metaphysics and personal Soul Journeys, I knew that we all have lived many lives. It seemed only logical that to get any lasting therapeutic results, I would need to go beyond the tip of the iceberg in this lifetime, and address and resolve problems at their source in past lives.

The Soul Journeys process was designed to provide a glimpse in full consciousness of the bigger picture of why we are here and how we can more easily navigate the dharma (higher purpose) of our life and relationships. It's important to note that hypnosis was not to become a part of Soul Journeys therapy. The person had to do this process in full consciousness.

While developing the fundamentals of Soul Journeys therapy, I'd only use more traditional methods with many of my clients. In so doing, I'd sometimes spend months or years trying to resolve certain issues with mixed results. With other clients, I'd use Soul Journeys therapy and more consistently get complete resolution in just a few sessions. It was obvious that within this form of therapy was a truth that any in search of deep therapeutic change would eventually have to take seriously. It even worked for those who didn't necessarily believe in past lives, but were willing to try it for results.

The unique therapeutic feature of Soul Journeys therapy is that once a core or key past life relating to a karmic pattern has been reexperienced and discharged, symptoms disappear and behavior changes almost instantaneously. This occurs without the usual interpretation and processing of traditional therapy. Clients experience a paradigm shift that may challenge belief unless you've seen or experienced it. It happens so quickly and naturally that even my own clients forget to notice at times. Often people who hear this have difficulty determining how or why it works in this manner, and so they understandably have doubt. When I recount stories of client experiences, they may wonder what else happened. They ask, *Was that it? After the session or sessions with you they were suddenly different?*

It can be challenging to explain how such paradigm shifts occur without delay after sessions. It may take a few days or weeks for even the client to fully recognize the extent of the changes within themselves, but it's not magical. We simply uncover and resolve the key past lives that cause problems in their present-life.

I believe the reason for this rapid shift is that suddenly nonessential karmic residue has been removed much like getting rid of unwanted baggage you've been carrying around your whole life. You don't really notice it unless it gives you problems. It's very much like finding a corrupt file or files on your computer and deleting them. Once the problem files or programs are located and deleted, the work is done and you just reboot the computer. The reboot phase is equivalent to getting a good night's sleep, which I always suggest to my clients after resolving traumatic past lives. When your burdens are gone, suddenly you experience a freedom of mobility and expression that you accept as *only* natural. Nothing is added, but the burdens you had carried are suddenly lifted.

Often I have to slow the course of change and transformation with sessions focused exclusively toward more traditional processing and discussion. This is to allow clients time to adjust to being suddenly free of previous burdens and to understand the implications of this new freedom.

I hope by giving some initial definition and explanation to some of the terms we will be using throughout the book, you feel a bit more prepared to embark on this journey with me. In the following chapters of this section, we will move toward a deeper understanding about what Karmic Relationships are, and the dynamics that govern them.

Let's begin . . .

chapter 2

What Are Karmic Relationships?

One Journey, Many Answers

Rochelle
3-21-02

Who am I, really? What are my dreams? What makes me so determined? Why do I respond to certain things the way I do? What do I really want? These are just some of the questions I have asked myself for some time and for which partial answers were finally provided during one session with Dr. Richards. My four hour, past-life experience was an awakening from a 48-year stupor. I realized so much about myself and for the first time in my life experienced profound understanding regarding my attitude towards particular circumstances, my dreams, my fears, and most importantly, my infinite capacity to love.

It was a past-life journey that took me to far away places in Europe that I recall yearning for as a child and well into adulthood. In that particular life I had been left with a large family that I ultimately murdered in order to escape my pain and abuse. I was later taken away to an insane asylum where I lived until I died, alone, in a bed by a window. This journey through a previous lifetime revealed iaspects of my personality that I had always been curious about and offered a plausible explanation to many of my personal issues, such as:

- Why did I believe that children of abusive parents are better off dead?

- Why was I so sickly and abused myself as a child?

- Why was my birth family so dysfunctional and cruel?

- Why do I appear to recreate certain painful life experiences, over and over again?

- Why do I find hurting a child, in any form, so horrific?

- Why do I feel enormous compassion for the mentally ill?

- Why do I get headaches and chest pains?

This past-life journey was unlike any journey I have ever taken—whether it was a made-up dream or an actual journey through a past life does not matter— I emerged from it a more integrated and balanced person. I am changed in so many ways but I am most assured of my abilities to take care of myself—to do whatever I need to do, in order to be happy. I learned that merely surviving is not enough for me—I truly want to seize my bliss and joy. I understand that I need never be abused, by anyone, anywhere, under any circumstance. I know I never have to hurt anyone again in order to survive. I understood where the pain in my head and chest may have come from and have not experienced the same level of discomfort in my body since the journey. Today, I have greater compassion for those who murder because I know there is a murderess in me. How can I know what motivates my fellow brother or sister to kill? I can only know that actions like murder and abuse are born of fear and insurmountable pain. Through the journey I gained immeasurable compassion and respect for myself, and feel freer to take chances and honor my inner voice. My soul is lighter and my heart is fuller as an outgrowth of this journey.

Lastly, very interesting and unexpected things have occurred since the experience. One especially curious event occurred 62 days after my journey. A long lost cousin, whom I looked up to as a child, contacted me. I had not spoken with her for 37 years and out of the blue she left a message on my machine asking me to return the call. I was not sure who she was—certainly never expected to hear from my cousin. I have not been in contact with any member of my birth family for over 30 years. I feel quite certain that my past-life journey gave me the courage to call her back and explore the possibilities.

We have spoken many times since that day and plan on meeting very soon. She sent me a photograph of a little girl that I subsequently framed and placed in my office. It's a picture of me, the only photograph I have of myself at that age. I can look at it and feel whole, complete, seamless and shameless. Prior to the journey, I genuinely detested looking at photos of my past—not anymore.

They say "the proof is in the pudding." Well, I really do not need any further substantiation that my journey, as incredible as it seemed to me at the time and for weeks thereafter, has altered my life in ways that I could never have imagined.

● ● ●

Years earlier, Rochelle had been through nearly a dozen sessions with a well-known past-life regression therapist. However, during my first session with her, I was surprised to uncover this key past life that was influencing her relationships with her husband, 9-year-old son, and many others.

As a mother Rochelle was happily married to a well-respected CEO of Irish Catholic decent. She was also the founder and president of a very successful Research and Development firm that required travel all over the world. She had extensive medical training, a doctorate in cultural anthropology, and a degree in comparative religion. A very attractive, expressive, and energetic woman, Rochelle was medium height with dark hair and very well dressed. As you might imagine, money was not a concern for Rochelle or her family. Although raised Jewish, she was of Latino origin. Rochelle wasn't the kind of woman who let anything or anybody become an obstacle to her success. She was very smart with an iron will, but also clearly enjoyed being a woman.

She had come to me because after years of building a successful company, her work was no longer as fulfilling as it had been. Additionally, even though she loved her husband very much, they had become merely partners and friends in their marriage. True passion had been gradually declining in their relationship for years.

She was also experiencing chronic pain in her head and heart area that was sapping her energy and causing frequent depression. Even though anyone could see that Rochelle was an energetic and passionate person in love with life and people, she found her sexual desire had shut down over the years. This resulted in questions regarding her karmic bond with her husband and her life purpose in general. Aside from the deep love she had for her son, not much else gave her personal fulfillment.

During Rochelle's first session, we found her as a 16-year-old girl orphaned to a large family. She was living in a farmhouse in rural England during the late 1800s and described the place as dark and evil. There were 11 people in this household including Rochelle. People and chickens were always in and out of the house, so she never had any privacy, even while bathing. Since Rochelle was not born into this family she was always seen as an outsider. The other children would constantly tease and torment her. They told her that she didn't have a mother and if she tried to leave she would die. This taunting agitated her greatly, making her sad, fearful, and depressed. The parents of the household provided little support or comfort. Rochelle retreated into herself by reading books and sitting quietly by the front door. There was a window there that provided some light and distracted her from the goings-on in the house. Her only other escape was occasional walks alone in the countryside.

After a few years of living under these conditions, Rochelle snapped. One evening she stabbed everyone in the house, starting with the father who was napping, killing them all. Afterward she stayed alone in the quiet house for days surrounded by the dead family members. Strangely, she could still enjoy the sense of peace and quiet she finally felt for the first time in her life. Today we might say Rochelle had a psychotic break and became homicidal. Before long, the local authorities came in a horse drawn carriage and took her to an asylum.

There she was given a combination of "shock-type" and drug treatments. (I later learned that camphor drugs were given in the 1800–1900s to induce convulsions as a treatment for psychosis.) During these sessions, she tearfully described how the chemicals left a horrible taste in her mouth making her nauseous and causing vomiting. She recounted in detail the torturous and primitive "shock" treatments they administered. It was a living hell for her in the asylum. In spite of this, as the years unfolded she found the will and desire to visit and assist other patients even less able than herself.

In 1874, when she was 33 years old, she died at the institution of a heart attack. Her name was Sarah Thistle. Research into death records confirms that a Sarah Thistle died in England in 1874, the year she gave during our session.

Although Rochelle had to forgive herself in that life for her actions, she also realized that she paid a painful price by experiencing years of confinement while being subjected to painful and torturous treatment procedures for her illness.

After this session, the chronic pain she carried in her chest and head went away. Her chronic headaches had led to occasional bouts of depression that previous treatments would not relieve. She also mentioned that she had always had a curious empathy for "crazy" people. And although she loved her son, more than anything else in life, news of women murdering children or children murdering abusive parents was somehow understandable and elicited her empathy. She now understood why.

Overseas business trips had grown very distasteful to her and she dreaded going on them. However, weeks following our session she returned from one and told me, "I feel so good, whatever you did I feel so integrated. I'm truly happy and feel so alive. It goes deep and is a real joy and comfort. My trip was not stressful and I was like in heaven. The things and people that used to bother me I found amusing and interesting."

Rochelle also shared with me that, "I feel compassion for people who I thought in the past were ludicrous. I can look at people and not have that harsh judgment, not have the thought that I am better, different, or more enlightened. I'm in a real comfort zone for the first time in my whole life. During this business trip I saw myself in such a different light."

Like many other clients Rochelle's changes came so fast that she wanted time to just take it all in before going on to resolve other issues and concerns. Our next session was mainly devoted to insight and discussion about how things had changed for the better in her life.

As you might imagine Rochelle's change of perspective had a significant impact on her marriage and the closeness she felt toward her husband. She suddenly had more joy and energy available to devote to the intimate side of their love bond.

karmic bonds from the past

Martin and Susan arrived in my California office and waited quietly in the reception area until I came out. They had only met in person for the first time a little more than a month before when they attended a health seminar. Actually, they first met on the phone when Susan had called Martin to inquire about the value of nutritional supplementation. While speaking with him for the first time, the immediate thought ran through her head to "keep this man on the phone." In her words it was "like I knew him and always had known him." She immediately had a feeling she would be in a relationship with him and the first phone conversation lasted for one hour. That night, Susan awoke from a very vivid dream about Martin, even though she had not yet met him physically.

After meeting at the seminar, and in spite of the fact that they lived in different parts of the country, Susan and Martin found themselves spending long hours talking on the phone and felt compelled to see each other as often as possible. They had come to me now by referral from one of Martin's acquaintances that knew of my *specialty*. Their only interest was to learn the mystery behind their powerful appeal for one another. Nothing therapeutic.

Martin, a medical doctor, is a middle-aged man of about medium height—very direct, cheerful, and self-assured. He shook my hand warmly and introduced me to Susan. Even though trained in traditional medical practice, Martin was open to the possibility that he and Susan may have known one another in a past lifetime. He was familiar with the concept of reincarnation, but had had no direct experience with it.

Susan, a nurse in a nursing home, is a gentle, soft-spoken woman in her early 40s. Fair skinned and with auburn hair, she clearly felt a strong devotion and comfort with Martin even though they had only known each another for this short period. Susan wasn't sure she believed in past lives at all, but she was at a loss to explain the intensity of recognition she felt for Martin, and she wanted to know why.

They were like two lovebirds sitting on the sofa in my office. After some initial questioning, I decided I would start the session with Martin. Usually when doing past-lives sessions with couples, I separate the two so that each has their experience apart from the other. In this case, it felt appropriate to make an exception and have Susan in the room since they were not really there for therapy per se.

Susan sat quietly in a chair away from the sofa as I began the session. Martin lay down on the sofa and closed his eyes. I wasted no time directing him through the Soul Journeys process into his most significant past life with Susan. He began to share that he was experiencing himself as a Native American warrior, standing outside his tepee, preparing for battle. At the entrance to the tepee stood his mate preparing to see him off before he left. Martin identified the Indian wife right away as Susan in this life.

The husband and wife hugged and kissed. Martin described looking into the woman's eyes, and clearly seeing she had the feeling, as he, that he would not survive this battle and return to the tribe. Theirs was a very emotional parting, but as an Indian warrior, he had to maintain his composure before riding into battle.

The next scene found this warrior in the heat of conflict, riding his horse and fighting alongside the others in his tribe. Suddenly he was struck in the chest by an adversary's spear. As he tumbled off the horse onto the ground, his dying thoughts were about the love he felt for the mate he'd never see again. With his dying breath, he cried out her name.

As you might imagine, by this time Susan, who had been sitting quietly in the corner of my office, was in tears. She'd been holding back the urge to sob as Martin unfolded this emotional and dramatic scene. Later, after the session with Martin, Susan told me that while Martin had gone into that past life and described their parting, she'd also had an overwhelming sense of being there as his Indian mate.

susan's side of the story

After Martin's Soul Journey, it was Susan's turn to experience a past life while he sat and watched. Much as Martin had, Susan went quickly into a past life. Her first memory of them in different bodies, and living in another time and place, began in Rome during the early years of Christianity. At this time, as most of us know, Christians met secretly in underground gatherings at night to spread the teachings because they weren't allowed to congregate openly.

Susan observed herself, late one night, as a young mother, walking down a Roman street with her five-year-old son after one of these gatherings. Unbeknown to the mother and child, the Roman centurions had discovered the group's activities. Soldiers were following her and the others. Guards stopped the mother in the street and arrested her on the spot. They separated the mother from her son and took her away to prison despite her heart-wrenching screams and cries. The mother and son never saw each other again. The mother was later put to death, as were many Christians during that period. Her son never got over the shock of losing his beloved mother when he was so young.

During this Roman past life, Susan had the clear realization that the young boy, who had been her son, was Martin in this lifetime. Because of Susan's Soul Journeys experience, Martin understood the reason for his intense longing to be with this woman and his willingness to overcome the obstacles of distance to do so. Susan later recalled two other lifetimes when she had known the soul who is now Martin.

The last past life Susan recalled with Martin was in the deep south of Mississippi. In that lifetime, she saw Martin and herself as black sharecroppers. Their names had been Millie and Elwood Johnson. The couple had a young son. Early in that life, people who hated Negroes had killed Elwood. His death had left Millie alone to take care of their property with the help of her son and some friends. She never remarried, and lived into her 90s, dying of old age in her sleep.

As you can see, the series of lives Susan and Martin shared together repeated a pattern of separation and loss. Is there any mystery why they had such a strong and immediate attraction upon first meeting in this lifetime? And why they had found it difficult to be apart once they'd been reunited. Their past life memories bear out the conventional wisdom that sometimes the simplest, most obvious explanation holds the greatest truth.

Martin and Susan are two clients who present classic examples of how karmic ties from the past cause attractions to happen in the present. After Martin and Susan's sessions with me, they both sat in my office with a deep understanding and realization about the nature of their unexplained and uncanny attraction to one another. Instead of just having the belief they had been together, they now knew of the deep love bonds they had shared in many past lives together. Neither Martin nor Susan had been surprised at the discovery of their lives together.

Susan later mentioned to me that what they both experienced was to be expected. She described the feeling of instantly being with Martin as he relived the Native American past life. She felt as if she could have completed the story herself.

From the first moment they met at the seminar, they had hugged and described the feeling between them as electric. From that day forward, they spoke every day. The couple seemed driven to pursue this connection. Every few days Martin, who had never written poetry before, sent Susan a poem about their relationship. Susan and Martin agree that somehow this was meant to be and they continue to grow and change together. Below is a poem Martin has allowed me to share with you that he wrote about the two of them.

Twin Flames

Two souls, forever linked.
Each searching for its compliment—
though knowing it not.
Two hearts, forever joined.
Each seeking Love—but finding only Love.

Two flames, lit by the One Eternal Flame
destined to merge with each other–
in time and in timelessness.

But first there is the agony of awaiting:
through the canyons of our minds we wander
on and stumble blindly through an often—
tangled maze of starless nights and sunless
days, while asking for some clue or road
to lead us to the truth . . .
but who will answer?

And sometimes they endure what Shakespeare called
"the slings and arrows of outrageous fortune."
And sometimes they endure living what Emerson
called "lives of quiet desperation."

Always seeking, struggling, striving
for answers to unasked questions.
Suffering a thirst that could not be quenched.
A hunger that could not be satisfied,
and an emptiness that could not be filled
by any of life's siren calls.

Trying to fill the void of not knowing,
while avoiding the feeling of not caring.
Because somewhere deep inside—they knew.

And then one day Heaven smiles upon them
and at a certain time and place
these long lost lovers meet
and once again reunite
in knowingness
of the Truth
that they
are
One . . . In Love.

As this book goes to print, Susan and Martin are still together and still commuting.

Karmic Relationships come in all shapes and sizes and all our relationships have a karmic dimension. Let's say you're having a hard time getting along with your spouse or significant other. The two of you square off and argue bitterly even though you've promised repeatedly that you'll talk reasonably and calmly. Most of your conversations these days end with both of you giving up and storming off, feeling hurt and misunderstood. You've tried everything to end these conflicts and have read so many self-help books on relationships that you could write one. You've watched the popular television talk shows and applied the advice relationship experts dispense. You've cried, prayed, and even visualized a better way of handling your relationship problems. Nothing has worked.

Maybe your relationship issues center on your children and how to communicate with them. Or conflicts swirl with a parent who is still trying to control your life. Maybe you just can't seem to work things out with a spouse, friend, or co-worker. You may see him or her as controlling, demanding, passive-aggressive, insensitive, uncaring, unsupportive, disrespectful, or just plain abusive. Buttons get pushed and then the two of you are right away off track to the point where you can't even remember what you were arguing about.

Relationships. We love them. We hate them. But who can live without them? Everywhere we turn, they're in our faces. So why do we so frequently find ourselves in relationship hell?

The answer to that question and all the relationship mysteries and puzzles I've ever encountered is contained in one five-letter word: karma.

karma is comprehensive

Even though many people think of karma as a bad thing, as in "you got yours," a Minnesota woman named Kathleen demonstrates the two faces of karma. Kathleen found a money clip of cash in the dressing room of a Marshall Field's store and turned it into the sales clerk. When the woman who lost the money tried to give her a reward, Kathleen turned it down. The sales clerk insisted that at least Kathleen should accept a box of Frango Mints.

Kathleen came home and put the candy away to give as a Christmas gift, but her daughter wanted to open the sealed box of chocolates and dive in right away. As it turns out, the box contained a winning ticket for a contest Frango Mints was sponsoring. Kathleen had won $10,000 and would be one of five winners going to Chicago as a contest finalist. The grand prize winner would receive $100,000!

Our deeds—positive or negative—come back to us with every bit as much certainty as the reward for Kathleen's generous and honest action. We don't notice karmic motion, though, because sometimes the effects of our deeds take lifetimes to return.

Because karma often remains undetected for so long, you may not realize it's most definitely affecting how you conduct your relationships. Karmic Relationships are woven from the threads, the karma, of past-life experiences with souls you encountered long ago and who are again players on your stage.

I designed the Soul Journeys therapy to help clients unravel the karmic ties that bind them to the past and limit the freedom to enjoy and learn from their relationships today. A Soul Journey can break the web of karma and help free you from the hell of love/hate dynamics.

what is the soul?

So many volumes have been written about the soul over the centuries. Who can say with authority what it truly is?

I define the soul as your true self or nature, the eternal part that continues on after the physical body dies. The soul is you as a spark of the divine. In the spiritual sense you and I, all of creation, are one, unified, and connected with all other souls. The soul is the divine essence poets write poems about and singers sing songs about. Invisible. Incredible. Invincible. The soul always survives. The soul remembers absolutely everything. It is the Superman or Superwoman within us all.

For me, working with Soul Journeys suggests the soul is that part of you which is unlimited by space and time. The soul stores a detailed record of every event you've ever experienced in your long unbroken past. In fact, to the soul there is no past, present, or future. Every event or experience from many lifetimes exists in the eternal now and is easily accessible by the soul. The statement that there is nothing new under the sun has deep significance from the perspective of soul. It suggests that everything there ever was or will ever be exists in the present. For a soul living fully in the present, life occurrences are like moving from one room to another in the great mansion of God. The mansion and its many rooms have always been there for us to enter if we choose them. That freedom to choose good or evil is the gift of the Creator. Eventually, we learn to choose our thoughts and actions wisely even if it takes thousands of lifetimes.

the panoramic view of soul

The soul's viewpoint is panoramic. During Soul Journeys you can go back in time, so to speak, and review events that escaped the notice of your conscious mind. Effects of these past events are still stored in the unconscious, and they continue to impact your life and every decision or choice you make.

The experience of a ten-year-old named Emily should give an idea of how the soul's panoramic perspective influences a person's life.

Emily's mother, Sophie, brought her child to my office in San Diego. Sophie had had a difficult and traumatic pregnancy. She wondered if this rough start in life had affected her daughter. Sophie had been engaged in heated emotional conflicts with her husband while Emily was in the womb. The pregnancy itself had been unplanned and at first, unwanted. From our previous conversations about the effects of thoughts, words, and actions stored in the unconscious mind, Sophie suspected that her traumatic pregnancy had left its unsettling imprint on Emily.

Since I had worked with Sophie a year earlier, she understood the implications of her difficult pregnancy on her daughter. Through love and understanding of Emily, she asked me to help clear away any prenatal trauma she might have been born with.

Some of the couple's arguments during Sophie's pregnancy had even led to her husband physically abusing her. This especially gave concern that she might have passed on patterns of conflict with men to her daughter. Sophie had noticed already that her daughter was fearful of men and seemed to have an unexplained anger or wariness when around them.

Fortunately, Emily was very comfortable and trusting of me and easily began a Soul Journey. The little girl rested comfortably on an open sofa beneath the window in the corner of my office while I sat in a chair with my yellow notepad and clipboard in hand. Emily took a few deep breaths and relaxed. With my help, she consciously—not in a hypnotic state—slipped back into the prenatal period when she was inside her mother's womb.

During an earlier interview Sophie had discussed with me many details of her pregnancy, but she'd never told her daughter about incidents that had occurred then. Now, as part of her Soul Journey experience, I observed as Emily consciously reviewed several episodes of conflict and abuse her mother had experienced during the pregnancy, including Sophie's thoughts and feelings about Emily's father. Like many reviewing the prenatal, Emily could give objective details of the things her father had said and done to her mother along with her mother's thoughts and feelings.

We focused mainly on arguments and fights that had resulted in angry words between Emily's mom and dad. Things like Sophie being called a "bitch" and told to shut up after her father hit her in the face. These were painful scenes for a young girl to recall, but they had been embedded in her unconscious. (As a quick side, this is the reason that the age of nine or ten years is about the youngest I'll allow anyone to delve into their prenatal or past lives. The material that is brought to consciousness could be too raw and painful for a younger child to process. You could say that some of these experiences are for mature audiences only.)

Emily and I began to resolve the points of pain and trauma her mother had experienced during the pregnancy. This process flows easiest with preteens and adolescents who just say what their mother is seeing, thinking, and feeling during the pregnancy without feeling the need to edit or analyze the events. The very act of reliving these experiences while fully conscious has the effect of neutralizing any emotional charge or attachment to the experience. The process simply brings the material up from the unconscious into the light of conscious awareness, where its impact quickly dissipates like morning dew in the noonday sun. It's a very systematic and exacting process.

I then guided her to recall just after she had been conceived. She described being in a heaven-like place with a "bald headed guy wearing a tan robe and weird slippers. The old fashioned kind that go up to your ankles." He was preparing her for this incarnation. He had been her teacher and was saying that it was time for her to go back to earth. From this heavenly perch, Emily watched her mother at her parents' home, helping them prepare the family's Christmas tree. Emily then stated that Sophie hadn't known she was pregnant yet. When I asked her if she was viewing this scene from heaven or from somewhere in her grandparents' house, she promptly stated that she had been in both places at once. Emily didn't realize the implications of her response to my question. She was simply and innocently sharing her perceptions.

This casual comment by a ten-year-old girl confirmed what I'd come to learn about the soul over the years. I have come to realize that a soul has the ability to have an expanded perception which is unlimited by time or space.

The essence of soul is Spirit. Since Spirit fills all space and time, soul must also potentially be omnipresent. In my understanding, the only thing that differentiates one soul from another is its unique experience from lifetime to lifetime. Without that, we would all exist as one in the uniformity of Spirit. We would be undifferentiated from this divine essence that is everywhere.

In that original state, soul is eternal with no real beginning or ending. The limitations we accept as a point of awareness are imposed through ignorance of our true potential as soul. These limitations result from our incarnation into physical bodies. From one lifetime to the next, we are constantly unlocking our spiritual potential through practicing, or the practice of, divine or unconditional love.

This dissolves the density of the karma we've created, eventually leading back to a state of true *Self* or soul realization. Consciously reaching this state has profound spiritual implications for us all.

Sophie later confirmed the details of what Emily saw that Christmas after conception in her Soul Journey. Remember that Sophie hadn't previously shared any of this information with her daughter.

On a side note here, over the years on three occasions, I've taken adult clients who were women back through the prenatal in an effort to uncover what was reported to be a "family secret." In each instance, these women were aware that their father had always treated them differently, with greater detachment than their younger siblings. They were all at a loss to understand why this was the case. For them, it was like their fathers withheld the love from them that he gave freely to the other children.

In all three cases, we discovered that the *family secret* was that they had lived all of their lives not knowing that their biological father was a man other than the father who had raised them. Returning to the conception, and reviewing the experience between the actual parents uncovered this. In each instance, when presented with this information, the mothers of these women admitted that it was indeed true. In one instance, after the truth had been uncovered during our prenatal session and before the woman could bring this to her mother's attention, her mother confessed this truth.

In this particular case, the mother had been under the influence of alcohol and had carried the shame and guilt about this incident her whole life. The mother had been married at the time and the biological father turned out to be my client's older cousin. I'll spare you the X-rated details of this episode, but from the soul perspective, my client described every detail of what occurred the afternoon of her conception.

Fortunately, in each of these three incidents the women experienced profound healing at the realization of a secret kept from them their entire lives. As a result these mothers and daughters were brought closer together in their relationship.

a panoramic view to beyond one lifetime

Continuing with Emily, I asked what she had done while waiting to be born. She said that she and other spirits, or "lights," as she called them, passed the time by playing tag in the clouds and open space above the earth. At other times, she would visit her mother or be in her mother's belly. Before birth she seemed to have the freedom to move about at will without restriction.

Emily also said that she knew her mother before in a past life in France when they had been kids and teenagers. In that life she had been taller than her mother, and they'd gone to school together as best friends. She said her mother had moved, but they wrote to each other and occasionally visited. Emily described that life as old-fashioned, and said that it had been hard for a girl to get a job. She said, "In those days only men were allowed certain jobs." Emily next recalled finally getting married and that she liked it. But while riding in a horse-drawn coach, she died suddenly as it tipped over. Right after her death in that life, Emily said that at first she didn't know what to do so she had stayed on earth for a while. In her words: "I barely knew I was dead."

After her Soul Journeys therapy session, Emily lost her fear and apprehension around men. Weeks later, her mother reported to me that she had been much different when visiting her dad. When Sophie's male friends visited, Emily now seemed more friendly and relaxed. None of the anger or attitude that she had displayed previously was evident. Her emotions had been based on a cellular transfer of the fear, anger, and physical abuse Sophie had experienced with her husband during the pregnancy. Emily's feelings toward men had started to generalize because while the baby was in her mother's womb, Sophie had started to think: "I hate men." Soul Journeys therapy enabled Emily to resolve the painful memories of her mother's pregnancy that she had been unconsciously carrying.

Emily's viewpoint while reviewing the events of her mother's pregnancy was extensive and comprehensive. As soul, she had a panoramic view that could identify all the surroundings and circumstances of her mother's pregnancy. Most of these prenatal details and memories had never registered, developed, or been activated in Emily's brain or conscious mind during the original experience.

At any point during a Soul Journey past-life review, we can freeze the frame, so to speak, allowing the soul to identify details of the experience from a 360-degree viewpoint. Details from past lives may have escaped notice when they occurred. But when a smell, taste, touch, sight, or sound, which is associated with past-life pain and trauma, is experienced again, it becomes a trigger for bringing back these same emotions into the present-life. Resolving such past lives allows us to live more fully in the present or *now*.

karma as energy

Karma is a form of energy. It moves, changes, expands, and contracts. Karma is actually stored in an energetic field that is like an invisible, interactive aura surrounding you constantly. Souls are constantly sending and receiving energy, expanding and contracting this field as they move through life.

You carry karma as an energetic frequency within your personal field. Ideally we are unwinding this karma that surrounds and constricts us like a cocoon of energy. This means that you have a certain vibration which can at times, be seen or felt as the aura with varying colors and intensities. The ability to see such energetic fields is a skill certain psychics or others have developed in this or past lives. No doubt, you have been in someone's presence and sensed his or her kindness, trust, wariness, anger, love, or power. These impressions you're receiving result from the energetic field that soul is emanating. Parts of this energetic field are in flux, constantly shifting and changing, depending on what a person is thinking, feeling, or with whom they are interacting.

Other core aspects of your karmic field are largely fixed and only change or evolve slowly over time. Certainly you've known people who have such rigid opinions, thoughts, and feelings that over the years, what they will think, say, or do in a given situation is very predictable. Their immutable thoughts, emotions, and opinions are the result of fixed karmic fields.

Karmic energy is either coherent and in harmony with universal cycles of energy, or incoherent and dissonant with the constructive flow of life. For example, when you feel in the *zone*, life is flowing, and good things are coming easily; your energetic field is in harmony with the universe. The *Force* is with you as you dance within the rhythms of life. It's a good day.

The karmic energy you generate carries your own signature and reflects back into your life in the same way you originally sent it out. This process is as automatic as the laws of physics.

Your karmic field draws you to certain people, situations, and conditions in life. This attraction or repulsion happens whether you like it or not. Your karmic fields can be either compatible or discordant with others.

I've found it quite interesting to watch karmic field action in my own life and that of others who come to me. Karmic fields pulling souls together or apart explains the mystery behind so-called coincidences.

For instance, twice while I traveled through Europe, the first time I got on a train, I sat next to someone who lived within fifty miles of my home in Southern California. The second time this occurred, the man I sat next to happened to live only ten minutes away from my home. Some would insist this is merely a coincidence, but even statistics would show that these meetings are highly improbable. Karmic energy draws souls, and is the glue that holds your Karmic Relationships together.

group karma

Many of your core energetic karmic patterns were established in lives past and carried forward into this lifetime. These patterns draw you to the same souls in similar situations over and over again. This is how history repeats itself from lifetime to lifetime at an individual, national, and sometimes global level.

Groups of souls that are fond of politics, the military, or battle, incarnate repeatedly over centuries in adversarial nations as leaders of political parties or the armed services, allowing conflict and war to continue to rage over the planet. You could say these souls are learning the lessons of power—it's use and abuse. It may take centuries, but similar patterns repeat in various ways with groups of souls all over the planet. Like players and coaches on a professional football team from year-to-year, different souls enter and exit a group, as they learn the lessons and move on to other lifetimes. The group itself has a slow-to-evolve consciousness established specifically for souls who need to learn certain lessons unique to that activity. And so, history repeats itself century after century.

For those who want peace on earth, I say, forget about it. There will always be souls incarnating here who need to learn lessons of power in some manner. Where are they going to go to learn such lessons? Venus or Mars? I don't think so. I'd love to be proven wrong on this, but from what I've seen of past lives, even being an optimist, I wouldn't bet on world peace. As long as there are dichotomies of rich and poor, weak and strong, my god and your god, there will forever be strife on the planet. This is the nature of duality and its expression, the yin and yang of life.

Souls are energetically drawn together, and unconsciously play out similar scenarios from their past lifetimes with each other and as a group. Wars, slavery, holocausts, renaissance, and reform periods all can be attributed to group karmic patterns that souls carry forward from one lifetime to the next.

soul journeys discharge karmic energy

When traumas from past lives cause unwanted reactive and repetitive cycles in your personal relationships, you can use Soul Journeys to review these lives and discharge the energy that holds such patterns in place. Core frequencies are deeply embedded patterns that souls carry from lifetime to lifetime. Core frequencies result in a person entering an incarnation with certain life themes in place. When an energetic discharge from core frequencies occurs, there is a paradigm shift in a person's overall life theme.

When you have a paradigm shift, you instantaneously release old patterns of thought from your subconscious mind resulting in the freedom to choose new ways of making decisions, interacting with others, and living life in greater harmony.

It's difficult, if not impossible, to express such freedom while under the unconscious influence of karmic patterns from past lives, which are causing you to hold fear and pain within yourself. Soul Journeys therapy resolves and releases the emotions tied to karmic patterns of energy. When this energetic shift occurs, you'll start drawing new and more desirable experiences into your life because now, you're no longer doomed to repeat the past. Desired possibilities for the future are finally within your reach.

A unique example of how this shift can occur from discharging karmic energy is the story of Laura, who came to me for marriage counseling. Laura was a dark haired, soft-spoken woman in her late 30s who worked as an administrative assistant. A friend had referred her to me. Laura was a practicing Catholic who went to mass every Sunday. She impressed me as a quietly pious woman free of malice toward anyone. Because of her Catholic beliefs, I used more traditional methods of therapy. Our goal was to help her get insight and perspective into a dysfunctional and abusive marriage. Additionally, her low self esteem made her feel powerless to face her husband or make any necessary changes. In spite of her requests he would not come in for marriage therapy with or without her. Being a gentle woman, the abuse and neglect she experienced was beginning to take a toll on her health. Over time as her sense of self-confidence improved, she fully understood she would have to make some hard decisions about her marriage without the support of her husband.

One seemingly unrelated concern that had been nagging her since childhood was her relationship with her mother. She brought this up toward the end of our therapy together. It seemed that Laura's mother had always disliked her intensely. She described numerous incidents from child-hood to adulthood when this seemed the case. Her mother was critical and disparaging of her to others in Laura's absence. For no apparent reason, her mother had treated her differently from the other siblings. It was so obvious that others in the family and even friends noticed it. It was like her mother hated her and even as an adult was always bitter and unkind toward her. Laura was at a loss to explain this as she had always been a quite, kind, and cooperative child and loved her mother. Unfortunately, Laura's mother lived across the country in another state, so even if she were willing to have her come into therapy, this was not an option. Upon hearing this my immediate impression was this relationship had it's roots in a past life.

With no other credible treatment strategy, I explained this to Laura and suggested we do a Soul Journey into a past life for the source of this conflict. Laura then told me she did not necessarily believe in past lives, and therefore had doubts. I then suggested that if she were open to the process she need not believe in past lives and could view it as a metaphor if she wished. She agreed and we began the Soul Journeys session. The focus was on the apparent resentment her mother displayed toward her.

Laura immediately went to a lifetime during the Middle Ages where she was with a small group of other women around a fire late at night under the full moon. Surprisingly, given her skepticism, the experience was very clear and vivid, unfolding naturally as if she were actually there. It so happened that the women were witches and this was a ritual gathering. Laura was the head of the coven. On this night another witch within the coven had challenged Laura for leadership and power over the group. Laura had anticipated this and met the challenge. With the aid of the other women, Laura had the other witch virtually killed and burned that very night.

During the session Laura immediately recognized her adversary in that life as her mother in this lifetime. When Laura realized what had happened in that past life she understood that her mother's anger and resentment was an unconscious residue from that past life. She could also forgive herself for inflicting such abuse realizing that her unconscious shame and guilt had made her overly passive in this life. This extreme passivity had actually attracted to her abusive personalities. You could say that her unconscious Shadow Self had abusive impulses and the only way she could see and experience it was through others. This was because it was buried so deep in her unconscious that she could not see it within her self. She had been willing to accept verbal abuse and neglect from her mother and later her husband because she carried this unconscious guilt.

Shortly after that session, Laura found for the first time the strength to make some difficult but necessary changes in her life. She called me approximately a month later to report that she had separated from her husband and was temporarily staying back home with her parents. Curiously she said that from the time of her past-life session with me that there was an immediate turn around in her mother's treatment of her. She had shared nothing of her past-life session with her mother, but even on the phone her mother was suddenly kind and accepting toward her. None of the anger, bitterness, and criticism was there anymore. She could hardly believe the change in her mother and called to thank me for the work we had done.

Because of this, she felt able and willing to spend time in her parents' home before deciding what her next steps would be. She didn't understand how, but felt that her past-life session had some how affected her relationship with her mother.

The paradigm shift resulting from Laura's Soul Journeys session had cleared and changed the energy dynamic between her and her mother. The release of Laura's unconscious shame and guilt had essentially neutralized that unconscious anger and bitterness her mother carried forward from their past life together. This happened because an energetic shift in one part of the system forces a change in the entire dynamic of a relationship. Because of this effect, when doing Soul Journeys therapy into past lives, a relationship can change significantly on both sides even though only one partner in the relationship has had the sessions.

Like one who is in a relationship with an alcoholic, when the enabler stops enabling the drinking in his or her partner, sometimes the partner chooses to stop drinking. It's all about shifting mutually reinforcing energy dynamics.

dealing with issues in a new way

Changes brought about through Soul Journeys are issue or dynamic-specific. Dynamics or issues in your life could be ones of abandonment, intimacy, aggression, physical tension, or pain. Dynamics express themselves as certain, unique energetic frequencies and are part of your karmic pattern. They're probably affecting every relationship you're in because they are your hidden wounds and as such, go undetected.

When a certain dynamic surfaces during a Soul Journeys session, it is discharged, and the way you have routinely expressed it shifts. This is what I referred to earlier as a paradigm shift. For example, if during a Soul Journey you recall a past life in which you were abandoned, fears of abandonment you've carried with you into this life and your relationships can dissolve. Sometimes, the shift is subtle but more often, it's quite pronounced. It depends on the intensity of the fear. A stronger fear will result in a more noticeable change. The shifting of your issues after a Soul Journeys session is a natural process and simply the result of letting go of unnecessary karmic baggage. As a soul, you've carried around this karma in your energetic field ever since the events occurred which caused your trauma.

The freedom and love experienced after releasing karma makes lives more joyful. Continually I hear the comment on how much lighter someone feels after a session. It doesn't get much better than that.

karmic relationships

Now that you have working definitions of what the soul, karma, and Karmic Relationships are, I can clarify why you and so many others haven't been able to fix those damaged, demanding, and disastrous relationships that have brought you to bookstores, therapists' offices, and workshops or seminars of every variety. You see, the problems you think you have with your relationships are merely the symptoms. They're the bells and whistles designed to get your attention. The relationships you've formed, whether they're satisfying friendships or your most frustrating romances, are like a long tail, swishing in plain sight, while the rest of the cat hides behind a bush.

Karmic Relationships are your cats in the bushes. These cats are the invisible aspect of relationships. Karmic Relationships are the eternal bonds you have with other souls. They transcend time and space and last beyond one lifetime. No matter how they look on the surface, Karmic Relationships are designed to help you eventually achieve unconditional love. At first, though, they may appear to be far off the mark.

Over the years, I've recognized that all my significant relationships have been Karmic Relationships. When I've remembered this principle I've tried to make the best of each encounter with a soul no matter what it might be, but many times I've forgotten that every Karmic Relationship offers a spiritual gift. Forgetting this basic principle meant that I went unconscious in the relationship as if in a dream for a while, sometimes leaving it with patterns and issues unresolved.

By exploring the levels of Karmic Relationships and identifying them, you'll take the first step toward becoming and remaining conscious of the influences that are building or destroying your friendships, marriage, living arrangements, or family situations. Keeping in mind that relationships are a mixture of many winds and much dust settling in from past lives and the present one, see if you can recognize the basic foundations of your most important relationships by using the information below. Then you can learn how to heal the hidden wounds these Karmic Relationships have buried in your psyche.

the souls you owe

The first level of Karmic Relationships is the *Karmic Debt Relationship*. It's characterized by the need to balance accounts from a past life in which you have caused harm, pain, loss, or damaged another soul. To be accurate, a soul is eternal and can't be harmed or wounded, but the bodies a soul assumes from life to life certainly can. In Karmic Debt Relationships the debt is often reciprocal; another soul has also done harm or damage to you, although there is an imbalance that isn't equally distributed between the two of you. Karmic Debt Relationships are often seen manifesting between couples or other family members when the two people carry a strong emotional charge in their interactions. Codependence is a common expression of Karmic Debt Relationships, where both partners feel they need one another in some manner.

Karmic Debt Relationships Questionnaire

Are you in a Karmic Debt Relationship with someone? Understanding this dynamic is your first step toward using Soul Journeys, finding balance, and having more peaceful interactions with this person. Think of someone with whom you have an important relationship and answer the questions below. If you've said yes to more than two of them, your relationship may be primarily one in which you owe this soul something from a past life.

- Do you find yourself on an emotional roller coaster of extreme highs and lows in this relationship?

- Do you feel an emotional addiction to this person in spite of reasonable and objective signs that the relationship is not healthy?

- Do you fear you'll never find a satisfying relationship if this one ends in failure?

- Do you constantly push each other's buttons?

- Have you ended this relationship more than once only to get back together and continue the same dysfunctional patterns?

- Do you ignore the sound advice of friends or counselors regarding how to resolve the issues in this relationship?

the souls who owe you

The next level of Karmic Relationship, which passes through from one lifetime to another, is the *Karmic Credit Relationship*. This type of relationship occurs between souls whose past-life experiences have left an imbalance in the spiritual accounts between them.

In another body, time, and place you may have given another soul a great gift, possibly even laid down your life to save him or her. Now, in the current life you've reunited, and in some way this soul will have the opportunity to repay you. This could be the history behind those people who donate a kidney or other organ so someone else can live, or the birth mother who gives up a baby for adoption to parents who will give the child a good home. Karmic Credit Relationships are the type of interactions in which people give and receive love and support in any number of ways.

For several months, a friend of mine led a coaching seminar with a group. One of the participants found out that he would die without a liver transplant. Upon hearing of his colleague's condition, a member of the group volunteered to be screened for compatibility. He donated part of his liver to the dying man, even though these two men hadn't known each other prior to their being in the same coaching program. This is an example of a Karmic Credit Relationship, which brought the two souls together, so one could help the other in time of greatest need.

karina's karmic credit

Another example of a Karmic Credit Relationship is Karina's. She described a karmic credit history, which reached back to early France and beyond. Forging karmic credits over several lifetimes with a woman who became Karina's Chilean mother, the woman would repay previous acts of kindness by bringing her to America.

Karina recalls that just before incarnating into her current life, she has the choice of being born in either Brazil or Chile. She chooses Chile because she's told that she needs to be raised by a certain family with a certain mother who will be instrumental in getting her to the United States. There she will have her next date with destiny and fulfill the purpose of her life.

Next, Karina views her life centuries earlier in France. She is a nun who runs an orphanage. She has a deep love bond for one of the little orphan girls in her care and does many compassionate acts of kindness for this child. That soul is now her Chilean mother in this life.

Digging deeper, Karina discovered that she and the soul, who became her mother, have had many other lives together which were challenging and painful. During these times, Karina and her mother worked through most of the heavy karmic bonds between them, and painful emotional charges were burned away. Only their love remained. This allowed them to fully support one another as mother and daughter today.

During her Soul Journeys sessions, Karina reviewed the life-selection process in which she'd decided who would become her family and she recalled part of her history as soul. This process helped her understand the dynamics of the supportive Karmic Credit Relationship she had with her mother.

Karmic Credit Relationships Questionnaire

Do you have Karmic Credit Relationships with souls in your life today? Answer the questions below to find out. If you've said yes to more than two of them, it could explain relationships that may appear to be out of balance because one person is giving more than the other.

- Are you primarily the receiver in this relationship even though you are willing to give equally to it?

- Is this a relationship that supports you even when you may neglect or take the other person for granted?

- Are you given unconditional support without judgment in this relationship even when you have somehow hurt or disappointed this person?

- Is the other person in this relationship willing to drop everything at a moment's notice to come to your assistance?

- Is this relationship so comfortable and easy that you have to be careful not to overlook how valuable it really is to you?

- Does he or she have characteristics and likenesses that consistently remind you of a beloved friend or relative who has died before this person was born?

the things you said you'd do

The third level of Karmic Relationships occurs as a primary basis for your interactions when souls have offered to assist one another in this life even though their karmic debts and credits are minimal. They share in the *Karmic Soul Agreement Relationship*. In this type of relationship, souls make agreements with each other during the inbetween-life state prior to their next incarnations together. Karmic Soul Agreements bring hidden opportunities and gifts of greater freedom and awareness with each new encounter and exchange.

One of my primary Karmic Soul Agreement Relationships is with my good friend, Tye, who I grew up with in North Carolina. It's become clear to Tye and me that our relationship goes back through many past lifetimes. Before we entered this life, we clearly had made an agreement to support each other in a number of ways. We continually look forward to visiting when Tye is in the United States or I am in Europe, where Tye lives.

As a lover of travel, Tye's pattern is to move to or visit a new place or country and establish contacts there. He then will invite me for a visit to explore and educate others and myself in an exchange of loving friendship. With Tye paving the way, I've made new friends all over the world.

Some of the characteristics of a Karmic Soul Agreement Relationship, and certainly ones that have been in my friendship with Tye, are that the two souls have a natural comfort and ease with one another. Tye and I don't need to do a lot of talking. Months can go by when we're not in touch, but when we see each other again, it's as if no time has passed.

Tye and I have discovered that our Karmic Soul Agreement Relationship spans lifetimes in China and Japan where we both practiced martial arts. It's an interest we've brought into the present and continue to share. Tye and I have been like brothers for many, many years. This is a Karmic Relationship I value and is much more interesting because we both realize it's been around for a lot longer than one lifetime. No doubt you have someone in your life like this, whether you realize it or not.

Karmic Soul Agreement Relationships Questionnaire

Could you be blessed with a Karmic Soul Agreement Relationship in your life? Use the questionnaire below to determine which relationships have entered this state of balance. Perhaps you have them with best friends, co-workers, or even spouses.

One point to consider, though, is that the Soul Agreements you've made with another soul aren't necessarily light and sweet. You may have a pact to give one another startling wake-up calls or to be positioned at a point in your lives where you will turn the other person more certainly in the direction that fulfills their life's purpose.

If you answer "yes" to more than two of these questions, consider that you may be involved in a Karmic Soul Agreement Relationship and take a look at how this is affecting your life and decisions.

- Does the person in this relationship intentionally challenge or stretch you to go above and beyond what you thought you were capable of?

- Does this person often recognize motives and aspects of your deeper self that you were not fully aware of?

- Does this person see potential in you that you haven't fully realized?

- Do you love, admire, or even respect this person for who they are and what they do?

- Does the bond in this relationship remain strong and familiar even when you've been out of contact for long periods of time?

- Did this person appear at an important point in your life and cause you to take a different direction than the one you intended?

- Do you have a specific religious, spiritual, cultural, political, social, or professional affiliation in common with this person?

the greatest love of all

The fourth level of Karmic Relationships is one that evolves between you and the souls who you reincarnate with over many lifetimes. I call it the *Beyond Karma Relationship*, because it is centered in a state of unconditional love in which the two souls are not constantly creating debits and credits with each other. Probably not many relationships can maintain a state of unconditional love, but I've found that by using Soul Journeys to release karmic charges and heal invisible wounds, people can come into that wonderful place where they drop blame, guilt, and judgment and begin to love one another without expectations.

You have Karmic Relationships for one very simple reason: These are the relationships that are the most likely and best suited to teach you how to give and receive unconditional love. And unconditional love is what it's all about. Unconditional love is literally what makes this world go around. Unconditional love is what we're here to learn from life. This happens more specifically through our Karmic Relationships.

Having unconditional love means being able to accept others without judgment, whether they're strong or weak; no matter what challenges they present and regardless of their flaws or preferences. Unconditional love creates a peace and tranquility in the soul that allows us to give compassion and acceptance to all.

Unconditional love isn't the same as the emotion of love, which often is sticky and demanding with expectations. Unconditional love is as impersonal as the sun's rays falling on every blade of grass without making any distinctions about which ones deserve or need more light. Unconditional love shines upon all life as compassion. It is fluid and doesn't show preferences.

Emotion is a knot of feeling in the psyche that is typically reactive. Most relationships stimulate emotional reactions. This is a far cry from the state of unconditional love. You've often observed your emotional reactions from this life, and these are the easiest to trace. The emotional reactions, which stem from previous lives, are invisible and cause you to have inexplicable divisions, preferences, and judgments.

growing into unconditional love

Christina, who is an artist, came for a session because she wanted to understand more about the fears which she felt were making the relationship with her husband Don less fulfilling. She started off our session by saying that during her morning reflection that day, she'd heard the inner voice of her spiritual guide whisper, "This will be the most important thing you'll ever do." She was prepared to understand why. Although she was married to a great guy, she couldn't allow herself to relax in the relationship.

During our first meeting, Christina recalled and released a great deal of emotion around a lifetime in which she'd been brutalized by the man who had become her first husband in this lifetime. These two souls had woven a complex web of karmic debts and credits as they took turns literally beating each other up from one lifetime to the next.

A few years after Chrisitina's divorce from her first husband, he died instantly in a car crash. By the time of his death, Christina had married Don who was very protective of her and her children. Her marriage to Don brought Christina much joy and self-respect. She described Don as someone who is consistently in her corner; giving her the unconditional love and support she needed. Yet as grateful as she was for it, Christina couldn't fully accept Don's love. She carried in her heart a lingering fear that he would hurt her.

Through her Soul Journeys experience, Christina realized that the fear came not from Don but from the previous marriage. By healing the hidden wounds of fear and distrust that had formed during past lives with her first husband and realizing that she'd worked through the karmic debts with him, Christina was now free to more fully experience the expansive, unconditional love Don offered. In this case, Christina wasn't able to have the marriage with her first husband grow into one that was filled with unconditional love. But she'd grown as a soul into a Beyond Karma Relationship with Don. Christina reported that her Soul Journeys session with me had resulted in a deepening of her trust, intimacy, and love for Don.

Beyond Karma Relationships Questionnaire

Are you in a Beyond Karma Relationship with someone? Use the questions below to determine if you've entered that blessed space where two people have grown to love each other just the way they are.

- Are you and this person comfortable being together while engaged in different activities for extended periods?

- Are you and this person happy and comfortably able to share time together with one another's friends?

- Are you proud of this person and who he/she is in the world?

- Are you able to talk about anything and freely, openly support and inspire one another?

- Do you feel that the giving and receiving is balanced and complete between you and this person?

- Do you complement one another in terms of skills, interests, values, and lifestyles?

Now that you may have identified some of your Karmic Relationships and how they are operating in your life, in the next chapter, we'll take a closer look at the secrets behind them. These are the hidden wounds, patterns, and life themes that are affecting every interaction you have with others.

chapter 3

The Secrets Behind Relationships

Five PRIMARY SECRETS ARE HIDDEN BEHIND YOUR ABILITY TO RELATE poorly or well to most of the people in your life. They are: invisible wounds, life themes, triggers, paradigm shifts, and Soul Groups. These unconscious elements—all related to your past lives, prenatal experiences, and/or between-life spiritual commitments—cause you to start up relationships, act out in them in certain ways, and end them for similar reasons. These five underlying aspects within relationships form the barriers and bridges between you and other souls.

As you will read in this chapter, the hidden aspects of relationships reflect on how they may be affecting your ability to love and be loved, to fulfill and be fulfilled.

invisible wounds

The painful exchanges you've had with other souls leave traces that you carry in the unconscious mind from lifetime to lifetime. These traces often appear as wounds in your present-life and can manifest in your physical body as places where you hold stress, areas where there are physical weaknesses, or even as birthmarks or physical deformities. On an emotional level, invisible wounds often manifest as strong likes and dislikes or exaggerated responses to certain people or situations. Hidden relationship wounds become present as attractions or repulsions to certain physical types or personality characteristics. They can rise to the surface in the form of fears of commitment, intimacy, abandonment, or rejection.

Most often, invisible wounds manifest in your over-reactions to things that push your buttons, even though another person would consider these same actions or words to be slight and insignificant.

Traditional psychotherapy would call for healing relationship issues by rooting out the primary sources of a client's problems through exploring childhood abandonment issues and previous difficult relationships they've had in this lifetime. The typical psychoanalytic approach could take years of ongoing sessions. But invisible wounds, stemming from past-life and prenatal experiences, can show up in a person's life today. The traditional therapist wouldn't know these issues are coming from something other than the current lifetime. From my observations, I've deduced that the most significant relationship issues often have deep roots that go beyond one lifetime's set of experiences.

As you might imagine, you could analyze your childhood and never get to the source of invisible wounds or any of the other secret aspects behind relationships that are rooted in prenatal experiences, past lives, or the between-life state. This is the power and advantage Soul Journeys have over traditional psychotherapy. Certainly more conventional analysis and insight has its place, and I use traditional methods at times with clients, but every tool has it limits.

Many come to me after going through years of traditional psychotherapy only to find that the results they were seeking required an intervention that could take them beyond the borders of their present lifetime into past lives.

from hidden wounds to patterns

Hidden emotional wounds from past lives create patterns that the soul carries into the present. These patterns are predictable ways you react unconsciously to situations. They can be functional or dysfunctional but they are reactive and automatic. An example of a Karmic Relationship pattern is the person who says, *I am always jealous of the person I love,* or *I am someone who gets betrayed when I trust others.* We all have numerous behavioral patterns. They're most challenging when they adversely affect our health, career, and relationships.

Karmic Relationship behavioral patterns get locked in through past-life experiences and are repeated and reinforced in your present-life. These past lives can contain a single trauma or a series of traumatic events that resulted in an invisible wound and set a behavioral pattern in place. Such a circumstance occurred to a woman who came to see me named Nancy.

Among other things, Nancy had no interest in having children. In her mind this was just a rational choice for a busy entrepreneur who had very little time to enjoy life. During our Soul Journeys sessions, Nancy realized that her lack of interest in having children stemmed from a past life when she'd been a Jewish mother of two infant sons. In a raid of her home, Nazi soldiers had snatched away her babies. She was herded to a concentration camp with many others and eventually executed. This left a Karmic Relationship pattern in place that said to Nancy in her present-life, "I am not a person who should have children. The unconscious message was that children cause pain."

After this Soul Journey and realization, Nancy could now make a conscious choice about her life and whether children should be part of it. She no longer had to remain stuck in an unconscious, reactive behavioral pattern that had been held in place by the energy from her invisible emotional wounds.

invisible wound repair

Behavioral patterns and hidden emotional wounds reside in your unconscious. After the soul leaves the body at death, it enters a between-life state. There, it can clearly and objectively recognize the behavioral patterns it exhibited while the soul was in an earthly body.

I haven't found that behavioral patterns, stemming from past-life trauma, are dissolved during the between-life state. Even though between-lives the soul can easily see the challenges it will face next time around, no adjustments are made to change or eliminate difficulties. From the perspective of the other side, souls view these karmic behavioral patterns as offering opportunities and springboards that will be useful in the next incarnation for gaining greater spiritual understanding and learning to love unconditionally.

After rebirth into another lifetime on earth, a soul has the opportunity to transform dysfunctional patterns into more helpful ones. It seems to be a spiritual rule that if a trauma occurred while a soul was in a physical body, it has to be resolved when the soul returns to reside in a new physical body.

So the cycle begins again. When the soul reincarnates from the between-life state to earth, it forgets the karmic patterns it agreed to resolve in this lifetime, and these embedded issues return to being unconscious.

Soul Journeys therapy intervenes into this cycle to help people recognize their karmic behavioral patterns by accessing the wisdom of the soul and healing the invisible emotional wounds buried in the unconscious and held in place there by karmic energy.

the evolution of healing invisible wounds

No doubt in the future we'll have technology to dissolve certain energetic patterns of karma and bring about emotional and physical healing of the invisible wounds that resulted.

I can envision machines that identify and measure the frequency and amplitude of karmic dynamics within the energetic field like a CAT scan or magnetic resonance. Your karmic field will be scanned, and frequencies of light and sound will be directed at specific areas on the body. When such flows of light and sound are directed at a complex in your body's karmic energetic field, deep-seated memories from this and past lives will surface, causing an emotional release. Like tuning a piano, the vibrational frequencies will be balanced, based on your ideal energetic resonance. The problematic dynamic or issue will dissolve, and healing of invisible wounds will occur. The paradigm shift in this case will probably be preceded by a quick and condensed review of the original trauma or traumas. It may also be accompanied by a spontaneous emotional release.

triggers

A second secret dynamic underlying your relationships are triggers. These are like unconscious emotional buttons that get activated by others or your surroundings. They generally cause an automatic response that can short-circuit your rational mind. Triggers typically have an exaggerated irrational quality about them.

In relationships triggers manifest as the things others say or do that cause an immediate reaction of fear, anger, or annoyance. One easy way to identify your own triggers is to consider the images on TV or movies that at once cause discomfort or upset you; sometimes even forcing you to leave the room.

Triggers can be a word, phrase, image, taste, smell, or touch. A good example would be the experience of a Persian friend of mine named Nasim. One evening while she was visiting, I decided to play the didgeridoo to give her an experience of the sound of this Australian musical instrument. After about 30 seconds of my playing the didge,

Nasim asked me to stop. She said that she simply did not like the sound.

Right away, I could see this was not just a casual dislike but also an exaggerated response. I knew my demonstration hadn't been that bad! For her, the didgeridoo was an instrument with a sound that she found unpleasant. I could tell that there was more to it.

I then asked Nasim if she would indulge me while I played the didge once more. This time, I wanted her to close her eyes, listen, and let the sound take her away in spite of her feelings about it. She agreed, and I played again.

After about three minutes she again asked me to stop, this time with even more anxiety in her voice. When I asked Nasim what she had experienced, she said that she had envisioned herself transported to a dark forest during the night. She saw herself as a very frightened man with dark brown skin and dark hair. The man was with three other men of the same appearance. They were all being pursued. Finally they stood, huddled together in the forest, terrified, and not knowing quite where to run or what to do next. That's when she opened her eyes and again asked me to stop playing the didge.

So where did this vision come from?

We can infer that Nasim had seen a glimpse of her traumatic past life as an Aboriginal male. Just the sound of the Aborigine's native instrument, the didgeridoo, had been enough to trigger Nasim's recall.

On the positive end of that spectrum, it's very likely that I myself have had an Aboriginal past life. Whenever I heard the sound of the didgeridoo on TV or in movies, I was strongly drawn to it. Later, at a Whole Life Expo in Del Mar, California, a couple from New Mexico had set up a booth where they demonstrated, displayed, and sold Australian didgeridoos. I could not stay away from their booth and finally purchased one. After about 20 minutes of a rudimentary lesson on how to play the thing, I took it home. Within weeks, I was able to play it reasonably well. Soon after, I developed the circular breathing method that allows one to maintain the continuous drone of the instrument without stopping for breath. It all came fairly naturally to me without further instruction. This familiarity strongly suggests some past-life connection.

Another example of this would be an acquaintance of mine who had a mother who was a symphonic violinist and a father who also was a professional musician. During his mother's pregnancy with him she rehearsed and performed a particular classical composition almost daily. Later, as a young flute prodigy, he found that this particular classical piece came so easily it was as if he had known it his whole life. He no doubt learned it in the womb. He went on to become an exceptional jazz flutist and innovator of the instrument.

As with Nasim, when you have no rational reason for an extreme reaction, given your known past, the triggers that cause you to go ballistic or as in my case, easily display a unique talent, may have their roots in your past lives. Even when there seems to be a rational explanation, based on your known past, the roots of a trigger may still reside in past-life trauma.

When activated, triggers have a hypnotic effect on you. The more active triggers there are in your psyche, the more reactive and unconscious you'll be in life situations. Triggers from past lives can result in your having judgments, strong unyielding opinions, and in some cases, self-righteousness. When you have a strong karmic tie with another soul, that person's very presence can be a trigger for an instant strong attraction or dislike.

Margaret's grandfather tripped a past-life trigger in her. When she was a little girl, Margaret had a strong, unexplained aversion to her grandfather and never liked to be alone in the same room with him. After further questioning I learned that Margaret had only seen him a few times during her childhood in a home with relatives nearby, so I was able to quickly rule out any possibility of child abuse due to isolation. Her grandfather died while Margaret was still a child.

By the time, Margaret came to see me, she said that in her relationships, she often wasn't assertive enough at stating her needs. Frequently, she would allow herself to be taken advantage of. She lacked self-confidence, and this affected her work and family relationships.

During a Soul Journey, Margaret relived a painful experience in which she recalled that her grandfather in this life had been her abusive, unfaithful husband in a past life. In that lifetime, the wife had died from a miscarriage resulting from her husband's physical abuse. In this life, the presence of Margaret's grandfather served as an unconscious trigger, drawing out the feelings she'd had about him when he'd been her husband during the previous lifetime. In her current lifetime marriage, Margaret often felt fearful and intimidated by her husband. The fear from the previous lifetime, when the wife had died at the hands of the abusive husband/grandfather, remained lodged in Margaret's unconscious. In this lifetime Margaret's strategy had continuously been to try and anticipate what her husband's response might be to her and only say things she felt would not ruffle his feathers. This is how she had acted out her invisible wound of secret fear.

The next week, after uncovering the trauma of that past life with her grandfather/abusive husband, Margaret reported she had increased her confidence and ability to state her needs directly and without hesitation After her Soul Journeys therapy, Margaret found it easier to say what was on her mind and no longer had an over exaggerated and automatic fear of reprisal. This type of resolution is often sudden and usually evokes amazing release. The paradigm shift can be immediate and dramatic.

energy releases and paradigm shifts

How often is it that you have knowledge or insight into a problem or unwanted pattern but can't change your behavior? It's in your head to make a change, but not in your heart. For example, after years, you may still grieve a loss or want to forgive a perceived wrong, but find it impossible to release the emotions that bind you. You may have even uncovered the cause of various fears, but still they persist. Why is this?

I've learned through doing Soul Journeys therapy that patterns of karma are held in place by energy that has been generated from memories of an original past-life or prenatal experience. This causes karmic patterns to remain hidden in the unconscious.

A karmic pattern or complex is actually a knot of energy, deep within the psyche, which transfixes images that store an emotional charge of pain or fear. It's almost as if the energy of a traumatic experience nails the image to a wall in your unconscious and holds it in place until you're ready or able to take a look at it. The pain you feel today is often based on a physical or emotional trauma that is still smoldering due to a major loss or failure from a past life. This energy, as you learned earlier, is karmic and part of the psychic baggage a soul brings into its current lifetime.

To change the karmic energetic pattern, you must release the energy. However, the energy is not released just by knowing about what caused it to be there. This is similar to any type of healing. For example, knowing your arm is broken and why, doesn't cause the bones to mend.

There are times when psychics or readers have told about a past life or lives that are the source of my clients' problems today. Others have gotten glimpses of their past lives in repetitive or recurrent dreams. Sometimes they will even get past-life insight from triggers activated by movies or other situations and events. This information about a past-life or prenatal experience alone is not enough to bring about therapeutic change.

In the account below, Stacy's paradigm shift of the karmic dynamic and the release of karmic energy caused physical and emotional healing to have almost immediate results. With a session of this nature, no further analysis or interpretations were required for her to heal and be free to make new choices.

Stacy had problems with her upper left shoulder and neck for most of her adult life. Although she was married with children, Stacy's relationship with her husband, Mark, was an ambivalent one. At times it was harmonious, but over the years their relationship had evolved into more of a partnership than the kind of marriage she had hoped for on her wedding day. In addition, Stacy often felt intimidated and put down by Mark's critical comments.

Although Mark was very different from her and the men she had previously dated, Stacy had felt compelled to accept and marry him. She'd been powerfully drawn to and almost overwhelmed by his strong, sure, and deliberate manner. Such meetings are signs of karmic cycles of attraction we have with other souls.

Stacy would occasionally drive from her home through a location in a neighboring community. When she passed through this area, she experienced extreme sadness and felt pain in her shoulder and neck. These sensations were amplified whenever she was in the car with her husband. Something about this particular location and Mark's presence were triggering Stacy's emotions and pain.

During one of our sessions together, Stacy experienced herself as a man, riding horseback on a snowy mountain trail in the Midwest. As a cowboy adventurer, he had two dogs that followed his horse. Stacy described herself in that lifetime as white, tall, and thin with a scraggly beard. She also said, "I don't see well. My vision is not that great."

The cowboy rode along a river, carrying skins that he would use for trading. He also concealed some gold nuggets in a leather sack.

The cowboy saw three men on horses approaching him. This gave him a bad feeling. Two of the men separated and positioned themselves behind him on either side of his horse. The third completed the circle by standing in front of him.

This third man asked why the cowboy was there. He told the men that he was trying to find an Indian tribe or two to trade with. The men claimed that the tribes were all theirs.

By this time, the cowboy's two dogs had started barking. The men asked the cowboy to show them what he carried, but he responded by saying that he needed to move on.

At this point, the man facing the cowboy looked to the ones behind and nodded. The man at the cowboy's right rear flank quickly rode up around to his left side. He stabbed the cowboy from behind with a long knife blade, slashing into the left shoulder. Then the man pulled the knife out and sunk it even more deeply into the cowboy who fell forward off his horse. When he hit the ground and lay on his side, his dogs circled him.

The men went through the cowboy's pack and then led his horse away. He drifted in and out of consciousness but could smell the river water nearby. Stacy recalled feeling cool air on the cowboy's skin and damp, hard, rocky ground beneath his body. She observed the cowboy trying to talk to his dogs. At this point, the soul was more out of his body than in it.

Stacy described a moment after the attack when time seemed to stand still. During this period, the cowboy reflected on the different choices he'd made in that lifetime. He flashed back to a woman named Grace whom he had chosen not to marry. He wondered what his life would have been like if he'd made a different choice.

As he died, the cowboy hoped the end would come quickly. His last thoughts were that he felt saddened by such a senseless act. He wondered if there is a God, why He would allow such people as these violent men to thrive. Consumed with a feeling of injustice and sadness, he slowly bled to death, surrounded by his dogs.

Finally Stacy saw her *light* body move out of the lifeless physical body, stand up, and walk toward the mountains. Looking back in this lighter, spiritual body, the cowboy observed the rocks, grass, and bushes in the little hollow where he had died and noticed the tips of his dog's ears.

At this point in her Soul Journey memory, Stacy realized that the man from this past life, who gave the signal to attack the cowboy, is her husband today.

As you might imagine, when Stacy remembered this trauma, it created painful and mixed emotions in her. But after reviewing the experience and discharging all the emotional, karmic energy that had been holding it in place in her psyche, she felt much relieved.

The next day after our Soul Journeys therapy, Stacy returned home to the Midwest. She deliberately went through the neighborhood where her shoulder and neck pain would typically flare and feelings of sadness had usually overwhelmed her. Amazingly she felt nothing—no pain, discomfort, or sadness. She said it was like a miracle.

Stacy realized that there was something significant about this area of the Midwest where she and her family had been drawn to live. After our session it became clear to her that this was the same location where she had been murdered and robbed in that past life as a cowboy.

For the remainder of that day and the rest of the week, Stacy was able to move her arm and shoulder around. She no longer noticed any trace of the pain or tension that had previously been in her left shoulder. And the pain never returned.

Stacy's way of relating to her husband also changed, once she drained the emotion that had surrounded her traumatic experience with him in that past life. Stacy now felt freer to be herself without fear or apprehension. She no longer subconsciously perceived Mark as dangerous because, after all, in this lifetime her husband wasn't trying to kill her.

Mark was also affected by Stacy's paradigm shift even though he had no knowledge of what had happened in her therapy session. He said that he noticed her increased self-confidence. This encouraged Mark to initiate a series of conversations with Stacy about how they could better support one another and their children. As the karmic cycles of attraction, based on their past-life trauma, started to unwind, they began to discuss how well suited they were for one another. Stacy and Mark were able to take a healthy and fresh look at their marriage commitment. After old karmic emotions within Stacy's invisible wound dissolved, resulting in a paradigm shift, the couple was able to find newer, healthier, more heart-centered connections with each other.

life themes

Almost everyone understands that history repeats itself, but the actual reasons for reoccurring patterns can be found in life themes—the next secret behind relationships. Repetition of patterns that have become life themes happen on a local, national, and international scale, but they all start with individuals who are doing the same things the same ways over and over again. These cycles of repetitive activities can be described as life themes. Both groups and individuals have them.

A life theme can be defined as the dominant gift and/or challenge you are destined to express, resolve, or manage in your life. For some, they are subtle and for others, life themes are more pronounced, but we all have them weaving through the fabric of our lives.

Life themes have both positive and negative expressions. In it's positive expression the life theme is the qualities, traits, and skills that are your natural gifts. In its negative expression a life theme can involve time after time when you challenge authority, experience loss or death, become abandoned or abandon others. Life themes are usually a mixture of positives and negatives that emerge as patterns of success or failure in different areas of your life. For example, former president Bill Clinton's life theme continually seems to be one of recovering from apparent failure or political disaster. Always the "comeback kid."

One of your life themes might be that you love movement and travel and do it often through the jobs you're attracted to. Business success may come naturally to you. Or you may have a knack for starting projects weakly but ending with great accomplishment. A life theme could be the tendency to attract into your life athletic, spiritual, or analytical people who love art and culture.

More challenging life themes are the tendency toward accidents, physical injury, drug addiction, workaholic patterns, business or financial losses, dysfunctional relationships and divorces, fear of intimacy, betrayal, and many others.

Life themes stem directly from past life and prenatal experiences that are buried deep in your unconscious but are still whispering messages to the mind and emotions.

Karmic patterns and invisible emotional wounds from your past lives hold life themes in place. On the surface, a life theme may appear to be caused by events in your current lifetime. But often, past lives are at the root of your life themes. Experiences in them have formed traumatic or painful unexpected losses that are fixed in the unconscious by emotions from a long time ago that have never dissolved.

Triggers, as mentioned previously, are red flags that identify fertile ground for areas of your life where life themes reside. When you find triggers and resolve the reactive patterns they cause, this creates paradigm shifts in your behavior and releases you from life themes that have been tyrannizing you. The undesirable life themes lose their control over your life.

In most cases you merely learn to live with life themes. But when they create ongoing problems for you and your relationships, they slowly come to your attention like when you begin to notice a constantly barking dog. With repetition and continued failure, you finally feel you must do something about them. As a mixed bag of positive and negative, life themes secretly underlie your Karmic Relationships.

mixed messages

Julio's experience offers an example of how positive and negative, or mixed, life themes get expressed in a person's life. He is the husband of Sally, who you will meet through her own sessions in Chapter 9. They came as a couple, yet each with marital and individual concerns.

Julio was from a well-to-do Mexican family. His father worked for the Mexican government in Mexico and in the U.S. While growing up, Julio had lived and studied in many places—Mexico City, Canada, Texas, Colorado, and finally Los Angeles. He had a positive life theme of travel, and his work today continues that pattern, requiring travel in the U.S. and abroad.

Even though Julio was very successful in business, he had a more negative life theme that involved conflict with authority.

For most of his adult life Julio had gotten into conflicts with bosses. On one occasion, he'd even lost his temper in a job interview. Julio seemed to attract bosses who would taunt or challenge him in mutually self-defeating ways. The reason I say mutually self-defeating is that Julio was a great manager and leader who could make a company very profitable. But his lack of diplomacy with senior management resulted in heated exchanges that often caused him to eventually quit. Julio would lose a job, and the company would lose a talented executive. This pattern played out over and over again in his life.

Two past lifetimes were primary contributors to Julio's life theme of having difficulties with authority. The first involved a past life as a priest in the Catholic Church. During this lifetime the priest incurred the wrath of a Church superior by making a decision that challenged his authority and favored villagers over the Church. His angry superior confronted the priest, who humbly stood his ground, knowing he made the right decision. The Pope was informed of the priest's actions. Although the priest narrowly escaped punishment, he was removed from his position and exiled. Years later, he died an old and tired man, feeling like a failure. The priest left that life, believing that it was impossible for him to function effectively within a power structure.

The second, yet earlier and most traumatic past life Julio recalled was when he lived as a master sculptor in Rome. He described himself as a large, bearded man with many apprentices. He had been very skilled and prolific, specializing in working with marble. He had a beautiful home adjacent to his studio. In that lifetime he was wealthy and quite well known, continually receiving commissions for large pieces from leaders and aristocrats.

On one occasion a powerful and influential leader, who liked to surround himself with servants and sycophants, summoned the artist to his court. The sculptor had never liked or respected this man but anticipated being asked by him to do a large commission. Sure enough, the leader told the artist that he wanted him to sculpt a huge statue of him that would be a testament to his greatness as a ruler.

Of course, the sculptor was expected to graciously say yes, but he stunned the leader by rejecting the request. The words seemed to come out of his mouth before he could even think about it. The artist had felt that to be true to himself, he could not deify someone who did not deserve it. He believed that his work was so good, it couldn't be taken lightly, and he felt a great responsibility for his creations.

On the way to this meeting the artist knew what would be requested of him and also suspected that this would be the last time he'd see the light of day.

After turning down the leader's commission, the artist was thrown straight away into a dungeon. In the dungeon the artist was shackled against a wall by his legs and arms. For the rest of his life he languished, growing old and gray. Over the years he watched others die in this prison and saw their bodies removed. The artist understood that, even if he had changed his mind and been willing, he wouldn't have been allowed to accept the leader's commission. A guard finally killed the sculptor by spearing him in the side while the man was still strapped against the wall.

Again, as in his past life as a priest, the sculptor died, feeling that his life had been wasted in failure.

As you can see, challenge and conflict with authority, which led to failure and death, were common threads in Julio's past lives. It's no wonder that having problems with authority became a life theme for him. In the current lifetime whenever Julio faced any conflict involving authority, the situation instantaneously triggered a chain of emotions related to his life theme. He was often caught wondering if he should defend a justified position while trying to manage his irrational, unconscious fears. His unconscious life theme convinced him that conflict with authority would eventually lead to pain, failure, and death. Because of the confluence of conflicting emotions, Julio's pattern had been to wildly exaggerate the situation and overreact to it in anger.

After our Soul Journeys therapy session Julio recognized how and why he'd repeatedly gotten caught up in his emotions and tense situations. Because he'd been able to dissolve the emotional energy of fear around his past-life traumas, Julio felt released from this pattern that had become his life theme. He could clearly see how he had gotten caught up in an unconscious swirl of emotion over easily handled and resolved differences with authority.

Julio's case is an example of the duality often expressed in mixed or widely divergent life themes. He had a life theme of being successful in businesses that involved travel but it was being compromised by his life theme of conflicting with authority figures and fearing the repercussions. By dissolving the negative life theme, which was stemming from past-life experiences, Julio was able to enjoy his natural tendencies to do well in business. He later reported to me that he'd markedly improved relationships with those who work as his superiors, supervisors, or in any other positions of power.

identifying life themes

Make a list with these four categories:

- Romance
- Work
- Family/Friends
- Others

In regards to "Others," some life themes involve physical health or the body. Some individuals have issues surrounding a certain area of the body and for this reason, I always ask where a person tends to carry stress, the weakest part of their body, where they have broken limbs or injured themselves, and lastly, what surgeries they've had in their life or if they have ever been rendered unconscious. Also, in the Others category, one could consider such things as fears, phobias, and other emotional reactive patterns.

1. In each category, consider one to three regrettably challenging and/or painful experiences involving others. Briefly summarize each situation.

2. Review each summary. For each of the summaries, identify which ones contain the same general life theme. Draw a circle around these summaries.

3. Place an "X" over each summary that identifies a different life theme.

4. Place a checkmark next to all the summaries that identify yet a third life theme.

Review the remaining summaries and see if a fourth life theme emerges. If so, place a star beside these situations.

Review all the events that you have circled, put an "X" by, check marked, or starred, and summarize the life themes they represent.

By now you should have identified three or four general life themes that recur in your life with love partners, work associates, family members, and others. These are your primary karmic life themes. They represent the cycles you need to break in this lifetime.

When you do the Soul Journeys process in Chapter 11, you can use one of the life themes to uncover the past-life roots of your Karmic Relationships.

Soul Groups

Soul Groups are the fifth factor in the secret or hidden karmic dynamics behind your relationships.

Just as you develop a group of close and trusted friends and loved ones here on earth, this same pattern holds true for souls on the other side. During your many lifetimes you develop deep love bonds with other souls and share lifetimes with them as frequently as possible. These souls are your spiritual family here and on the other side.

Woven through your lifetimes are loosely or tightly interlacing karmic ties that you share with your Soul Group, or cluster. On the other side of death, it is with these souls that you make agreements to play strategic roles involving love, support, challenge, entertainment, empowerment, and advise. Soul Group members interact with each other in these ways for lifetime after lifetime within family, business, political, religious, and many other types of groupings.

It is said that when you marry a partner you marry his or her whole family. The same holds true for Soul Groups. When you engage in a Karmic Relationship with another, both of your Soul Groups overlap. You become part of a much larger energetic karmic system that affects everyone in that system directly or indirectly. Depending on how you show up, your influence can have a stabilizing effect on the group or not. It's all up to you.

No doubt you've had the experience of meeting some-one for the very first time and feeling a strong recognition or a casual familiarity with them. These encounters usually lead to bonds and shared experiences that span a certain period or can last an entire lifetime. Deep love and affinity results in bonds that are forged before each incarnation.

Soul Groups also carry forward similar life themes from lifetime to lifetime. As I mentioned earlier, this is how history repeats itself and can result in valuable uses and regrettable abuses of power and knowledge on a small or large, national, or global scale.

The souls within these groups have history together, which is based on a mixture of successes and failures with each other in past lives. When trauma is involved with their failures, the emotional charge from such events carries forward from one life to the next within the group's consciousness. This emotional karmic charge or energy acts on the Soul Group just as it works within an individual. As a result, you could say that each Soul Group has its own unique personality and ways of handling conflict, opportunities, or mistakes. Stored karmic energy sets up a pattern of repetition that draws the group into cycles of activity. Examples are all around us, especially when we consider the behavior of companies like Microsoft, Apple, General Motors, Enron, or the Democratic and Republican parties.

maria's soul review

I've found that the period between-lives is equally, if not more significant than past lives in charting the continued progress of evolving souls.

An experience a woman named Maria had during a Soul Journey should provide deeper insight into the possibilities of the between-life state. As a soul before incarnating, Maria made numerous, very significant choices and gained many insights during the between-lives period.

Maria and I had reviewed a lifetime when she died early as an adult male. On the deathbed, the man had been surrounded by his mother and several other family members and relatives. In the end, it was a peaceful death he experienced as a relief after a long illness.

In her present life, Maria had been an engineer and draftsperson working in her father's firm. As a result of several surgeries that had removed her thyroid and parathyroid gland, she developed chronic fatigue and later fibromyalgia. Eventually she had to stop working and go on disability.

Married, it took all the energy Maria had to maintain a household and be a loving wife to her husband. We had been through several Soul Journeys sessions in an effort to relieve some of her physical and emotional stress and pain.

During the following session we ventured in the between-life state just prior to her present lifetime to uncover some insights and bring greater understanding into her present-life circumstance. Our session went like this.

C: What do you see as you leave the body?

M: I float upward and see clouds and colors and have a sensation of freedom and joy.

C: As you continue, what do you see next?

M: I start to see land and greenery in a beautiful garden like setting with rolling hills. I'm coming down to it.

C: After you come down, what do you see?

M: I see a structure. A stone building and walk toward it.

C: Describe the building you see.

M: It's stone with a beautiful walkway leading toward it. There are beautiful carved doors and windows at the front. I hesitate to go in trying to absorb it all. There is a bench outside so I sit on it.

C: What do you see as you sit there?

M: I see beautiful gardens and hills. Now I get up and open the door. It's quiet inside with beautiful rugs on the floor. Someone is sitting at a desk.

C: How does this person appear?

M: [It's] a slender male with black hair and blue eyes. He waits for me and I go over to speak to him.

C: What do you and he say?

M: I ask him what is this place and he says it's a hall of records. I tell him I want to see my records. He directs me to a particular room and says they will bring them to me.

C: What do you do once in the room?

M: I sit and wait for the records.

C: How does the room appear?

M: It's a beautiful room with gemstone walls. The gemstones are formed into tiles on the walls in colors of blues and greens. There's also a couch and a chair with a desk in the room. Nearby there is an octagonal window on the wall. The window looks like clear-leaded glass.

C: What do you do next?

M: I go through my records. They are on a creamy colored paper in a book like form.

C: What do you see?

M: I see lots of different past lives, good ones and bad ones, like movies. The book shows me pictures that come alive like movies as you look at them.

C: Describe the lives that you see?

M: I see one life where I wasn't very nice. I was a male in that life that wasn't a very good person. I was angry and resentful and took from people as I pleased. I killed and robbed banks and was not very nice. I'm disgusted with that one.

C: What else do you see?

M: Another life is more beautiful. I was a society lady in France. Things were much more beautiful in that life and I had everything I wanted. People also loved me and I loved them. I had servants and a wonderful husband.

C: Continue.

M: I look at another life in china as a woman. I was tall, slender and nice looking for a Chinese woman. I had to work hard in the rice patties. I love the simplicity, hard work, and endurance I had in that life. I didn't mind it much and could be content to do what I needed to do. I wanted more, but I was still content.

C: And the next life you see?

M: I was a black boy that got killed by a dog because I stole bread.

C: How did this happen?

M: I was in the main house and was hungry. I stole some bread and ran into the woods to eat it. The master brought a pack of dogs looking for me. I was eleven years old.

C: When did you die in that lifetime?

M: I died in 1781.

C: What else do you see in the records?

M: Looks like there are some choices to be made.

C: How do you know this?

M: I came to a page where it said "Choices" and I start reading it. They are choices for your next life.

C: What do you see?

M: First I see a male gambler, a terrible life to have to live. It's visually imparted to me. Next I see I could have come back as a cripple female.

C: Are there any other choices?

M: Nothing else comes from that page anymore. I close the book and sit there thinking
about the choices. None of them seemed
very good because of the life when I was a
robber and had hurt many people. I had to
experience something difficult.

C: Continue, what do you do next?

M: A short, older gray haired gentleman has
come in to talk to me. He is loving, understanding and sympathetic. Nothing is harsh
about him. He asks me what I would like to
do. I say none of these are appealing to me.
He says maybe you can come up with something. I then say well, let me think about it
for a while.

C: Continue.

M: I'm allowed to sit down and come up with a
life that would give me a challenge. I write my
ideas down. The lives presented as choices
had a challenge. I settle for physical weakness
as a woman but not to the point of being
immobile. The life would have difficulties in
different areas that would give me challenges.

C: What happens once you develop a profile?

M: The older gentleman returns and takes me,
along with my ideas, to make a more formal
decision for that lifetime. He takes me into a
room with a few different other people, a
hierarchy, so that they can agree or dis-
agree.

C: How many are in the hierarchy?

M: There are ten of them; all older men and one
woman. They agree.

C: Continue.

M: They said that now I can be dismissed and go into a vacation time. I get a relaxing and peaceful atmosphere for some time.

C: Where do you go?

M: I go to a quaint little city that reminds me of a European village. People are welcoming me and they make me feel loved. I'm staying in a beautiful cottage with a creek nearby that makes a lovely sound. The cottage is decorated very quaint and old fashioned and is warm and cozy.

C: Is anyone you know in this village?

M: My dad and sister in this life are there and they come over to visit. They heard I was in the area. My father was my child at one time (in an earlier life). My sister was one of my aunts from the life I just left.

C: What do you do in this village?

M: I visit with people in the village and surroundings. They all seem to be familiar acquaintances.

C: What else do you do?

M: There are lots of books and I like to read so I spend lots of time reading.

C: What kind of books do you read?

M: I read books on science, astronomy, poetry and novels. It's a beautiful area so it's nice to take walks around there and look at all the beautiful scenery. I also go to others homes, visit and chat. There are shops and people create things and show them.

C: Do you use money?

M: You kind of trade for them.

C: Trade what?

M: You trade whatever you have to offer. I trade my knowledge of questions people ask me and that I can answer.

Maria's experience is typical of the initial stages of review after an earthly incarnation. However, there are infinite variations on how the between-life stage is experienced by different Souls. In later chapters you will see how the experience between lives varies. This seems to be based on the awareness, beliefs, expectations, and past-life history of each individual Soul.

In Chapter 4, you will discover how the *Shadow*, a key to self-realization, is drawn to you through your Karmic Relationships. The Shadow is a concept taken from Jungian psychology, but it has more literal significance when considered from the perspective of past lives.

Through Soul Journeys you'll be able to observe how in the past you actually were your own worst nightmares and can now be released from them.

chapter 4

The Relationship Revolving Door

IN YOUR RELATIONSHIPS, ESPECIALLY THOSE THAT ARE FULL OF RANCOR, you may analyze who did what and why for a whole lifetime. But not much will change until you understand and accept the principle of karma and how Karmic Relationships are playing out in your life. Until you have a greater understanding of karma and are free to express love without judgment, you'll remain stuck inside the revolving door of relationships.

As we move into this chapter, see if you are experiencing any past life aspects in your relationships like the ones listed below. If you say "yes" to four out of the seven statements, you are in a Karmic Relationship based on strong *Shadow* components from past lives.

- Is the chemistry or physical attraction to one another intense in spite of strong differences and conflicts you have when you're together?

- Do you feel addicted or overly attached to your partner and find yourself unable to let go of him or her?

- Have you broken up several times but are continually drawn back together out of fear or for the wrong reasons?

- Are you not inspired to be your best and reach to your full potential in the relationship instead feeling trapped and limited?

- Do you feel fearful or unable to share your true thoughts and feelings in this relationship?

- In spite of yourself and going against your better judgment, are you unable to say no to him or her?

- Would you describe this relationship as a love/hate roller coaster in which your partner knows exactly how to push your buttons or reel you back into it?

One of the most common and sure ways to reach your full potential in love and self-awareness is by building relationships with others. Karmic Relationships offer opportunities for you and others to resolve long-standing karmic patterns that hold you back from becoming fully developed as a human being and as soul.

I've learned through clients as well as from my own spiritual experiences and studies that the reasons we incarnate repeatedly are to learn unconditional love and compassion and to give service to others and the world. It figures that the process of loving unconditionally, as God loves, begins and grows through our Karmic Relationships with others. We've earned our Karmic Relationships, and God uses them through the medium of karma to teach us important spiritual lessons.

By now you probably realize that your karmic patterns have deep roots and often carry much energy that influences your actions and behaviors. The problem is that karmic patterns don't change until you discharge the energy that is holding them in place and see the lessons contained within your karmic experiences. Over and over, not knowing why this happens, you will be drawn to the same type of partner until you somehow break the hold of a karmic pattern. The energy of your karmic patterns is conditioning you to make relationship choices.

This process isn't merely a matter of expectations. For example, it's not only that a person who expects to be abused in a relationship gravitates toward an abuser to fulfill those expectations. Karmic patterns, embedded in the unconscious, are running the show. They move abusers and abused from previous lifetimes back together as surely as the laws of physics govern physical energy.

Even though you may try to override a karmic pattern, it continues to surface in your relationships. This is why I call Karmic Relationships a revolving door. Souls incarnate time and again, going round and round, entering and exiting their relationships as different bodies but never really leaving the house that their karma built.

opposites and like do attract

So how do you resolve the karmic ties that keep drawing you to choose the same type of partners?

What are your karmic patterns?

Do you notice yourself choosing partners who are emotionally unavailable? Controlling? Passive? Addictive? Obsessive? The list is endless, but somehow, does the same type of person keep showing up in your life?

Why is this?

Two principles come into play here. You've heard these old adages many times before but as it turns out, karmicly, they are true. One principle is that *like attracts like*. The other is that *opposites attract*.

Those you attract and who are attracted to you are emotional mirrors to your own level of emotional maturity. Their issues are your issues. Their challenges are your own. Upon close examination you'll be able to observe that the needs, desires, and fears of the people you are attracted to are very similar to yours. Like attracts like.

On the other hand the expression of their needs, desires, and fears may be the opposite of how you express yours. If you fear emotional hurt and pain in relationships, this may cause you to be overly needy or too willing to please. A person who is attracted to you may have the same fear of being emotionally wounded but expresses it through an unwillingness to get too intimate or really open up. The fear is the same, but its expression is the opposite.

If your karmic pattern has resulted in an invisible wound, dynamic, or life theme of being emotionally insecure in relationships, a person you're attracted to who has the same karmic pattern may express insecurity by hiding it and being overly aggressive and controlling. The same holds true for any issue—dependence/independence, aloofness/friendliness, and optimism/pessimism—the list goes on and on. Any extreme or reactive expression of an emotional pattern, be it positive or negative, reflects some insecurity.

the shadow

The subconscious attraction or negative reaction to similarities between others has symbolic significance in Jungian and popular psychology. Dr. Carl Jung, the famous Swiss psychiatrist, called the Shadow the qualities you see in others, which you automatically dislike in them. The Shadow is composed of the characteristics or traits within yourself that you are either ashamed of, try to hide, or dislike and suppress. The universe, the Life Force, Spirit, or however you refer to the intelligence that operates all of creation, will not be fooled by what you try to hide from others. At some point, the universe will force you to face Shadow aspects of your personality, because you'll draw people into your life that will mirror them for you.

Shadow qualities can show up in love relationships, among your friends, work associates, or anyone in your circle of contacts. Recognizing and accepting your Shadow is so important that Jung said that integrating the Shadow is the first step toward *self-realization.*

So how do you integrate the Shadow and begin the journey to self-realization?

In traditional psychology integrating the Shadow can take many months or years of therapy, depending on the intensity of Shadow repressed material. With Soul Journeys into past lives you will have a more direct way of recognizing and integrating the Shadow aspects of your personality and relationships. This can happen in a single session.

When Shadow material is so intense and deeply buried in the unconscious that it seems immune to honest reflection and examination, it may be rooted in past lives. But not every Shadow element has a past-life origin.

Sometimes your Shadow projections onto others are merely based on subconscious opinions and judgments that were formed in your childhood. They are hand-me-downs from your family of origin and others who had a strong influence on you. You have merely taken ownership of these judgments and accepted them as part of your identity. These types of Shadow projections are represented in generalized statements such as: You can't trust lawyers, used car salesmen, or politicians. Others are racial stereotypes. You can often face inherited Shadows with the light of truth and dissolve them. Author, Debbie Ford, has written an excellent book on this manifestation of the Shadow, entitled *The Dark Side of the Light Chasers: Reclaiming Your Power, Creativity, Brilliance, and Dreams.*

On the other hand, when you're strongly self-righteous about a particular judgment or opinion of another and assume it to be a truth you must defend, you may be facing a mirror into your own past lives. A statement I've found to be true and now live by is *judge it and it's yours.* This cuts to the core of many of the challenges we bring on ourselves. When we judge another, we automatically set ourselves up for experiencing their challenge. This is an easy way of getting in line to make someone else's karma your karma.

Judge another and sooner or later you will find yourself walking in his or her shoes.

past-life shadows

Early in life I developed the opinion that I couldn't trust authority. I repeatedly confirmed this belief by observing and identifying failings and abuses of authority in others. I saw in them what I expected to see.

Later, I came to realize that underlying my distrust of authority was a fear that stemmed from my past-life traumas at the hands of authority and the past lives in which I had abused power and authority. I eventually had to forgive myself for those times when I'd mishandled power. Distrust of authority in this lifetime had been my way to subconsciously recognize my Shadow in others.

Now I watch objectively as others use or abuse power and authority. I don't judge them, but I do recognize if the results of their actions are constructive or destructive. Distrust and fear of authority are no longer my issues, so I don't react to abuses or draw them into my life. You could say that the universe finally got through to me.

Typically the Shadow is seen symbolically as a part of yourself that is projected out and onto others. When you Soul Journey into past lives, the Shadow is no longer a concept or a symbol. You get to experience your Shadow Self literally and directly. Like it or not, you find that you actually *were* your Shadow in past lives. To reexperience your Shadows directly is a priceless way of recognizing and accepting previously hidden qualities, traits, or flaws in yourself and others.

Past life recall of your Shadow also allows you to transcend judgment and neutralize your reactions when the relationships in your life today mirror them. With this neutralization comes the freedom to no longer need to attract or draw negative people and relationships into your life. Choosing to maintain neutrality in the face of conflict becomes a form of karmic self-defense. By this I mean, you are no longer drawn into unwanted karmic bonds with others. When they do show up in your orbit, you can see them without judgment for who and what they are.

kirsten and dave

Kirsten is a classic example of a person meeting a Shadow Self from a past life. She has never liked passive, self-sacrificing, dependent women. When movies or television portrayed this type of female, Kirsten became very annoyed and would often get up and leave the room. To some extent this negatively impacted Kirsten's relationship with her mother, whom she viewed as having the characteristics she so despised.

Kirsten herself valued strong, independent, active, and dynamic women who made their own decisions and lived by them. Kirsten's Shadow Self, hidden in her subconscious, was the passive, dependent, self-sacrificing type of woman that she didn't like and was determined never to be. When she talked about her judgmental attitude toward submissive women, I could see that this attitude was an obvious projection of Kirsten's subconscious fear. In fact, fear lay at the core of Kirsten's rejection of passive femininity.

Kirsten was an attractive, middle-aged brunette of average height. Very athletic with energy to spare, the sparkle in her eye and youthful demeanor belied her age. She could easily have passed for ten years younger. She had had a challenging relationship with Dave, her husband of seven years. They'd met and fallen in love quickly, feeling that they were destined to be a couple. Theirs was a magnetic attraction from the start.

Shortly after they married dynamics emerged in the relationship that frustrated them both. Dave was strong, athletic, organized, and systematic. He had a firm sense of how things should be. Unlike his wife, Dave didn't express affection openly.

Kirsten was more of a free spirit—passionate and spontaneous. An artist and graphics specialist by trade, she enjoyed leaving room in her life for diversion and impulse. Kirsten viewed her husband as being somewhat detached, controlling, and restrictive. One interest that Dave and Kirsten shared, though, was a need for having spirituality in their lives.

Kirsten vacillated between being dependent on Dave by letting him dominate and limit her, and at other times, breaking free of his perceived restrictions to act more self-directed. Their ongoing conflicts had caused the couple to separate three times during their seven-year marriage. This was partly due to Kirsten's desire to be independent and additionally because of her attraction to other men.

Kirsten and Dave had remained friends throughout their marriage and separations but they finally divorced. Toward the end of their marriage, Kirsten had a dream insight into a previous lifetime that she believed had a direct bearing on her current life. Later, during a session with me, Kirsten did a Soul Journey to further clarify and resolve the karmic issues that had emanated from this past life.

kirsten's shadow

Kirsten verified during her past-life Soul Journey that she had been a farmer's wife who had been unfulfilled and unhappy. In that life she'd often dream of being in a more satisfying relationship with another man.

The scene of Kirsten's past-life memory began as the woman she used to be standing in the kitchen of her home during pioneering days in Kentucky. She was cleaning up and preparing food. She wore a blouse and a long, drab-colored skirt.

Kirsten described the woman as miserable, trapped, empty, and unable to tolerate her life. Her passivity, dependence, and strong religious beliefs kept her from even considering leaving that marriage. She longed to have a better life with a loving husband and children. Sadness surrounded her as she wondered how God could have given her such a miserable life.

The woman's husband was the strong, quiet type who completely dominated her. She had her responsibilities on the farm with domestic activities, and her husband did the rest of the chores.

Because there was such a lack of love and affection in this marriage, the couple often argued. On this day, her husband had walked into the kitchen and suspiciously accused her of having an affair. Since she often had fantasized about how happy her life would be with another man, her husband's words made her feel guilty. Therefore, she didn't openly deny having an affair, even though she never had been unfaithful. Her strong religious beliefs suggested that the thought was just as bad as the action.

As their argument heated up, her husband began pacing angrily around the house. He ran his hand through his hair while raging jealously. He called his wife a whore and said he wished he'd never married her. Their fight became more intense. The wife started to fear her husband's wrath.

Finally in a moment of uncontrollable anger, he grabbed her by the wrists and yelled, "You forced me to do this. You betrayed me." He dragged her out of the house, while she kicked and screamed at him. She saw him looking around for a shovel and realized what he had in mind. She fought with all her strength to get away from him.

Her husband first knocked her unconscious with his fist. Then he began to dig a grave. He threw her body into the hole and started to shovel dirt over her. She regained consciousness and screamed in panic and terror just as he was covering her face. Choking, she could no longer breathe. She died of suffocation from being buried alive.

Afterward, her husband wept by her grave.

karmic connection

As Kirsten relived that past life, she realized that the farmer, who had been her husband, was her husband Dave in this life. In her marriage with Dave, she had some of the same feelings of sadness and being trapped as she had had in the pioneer days.

Kirsten and Dave's marriage was a Karmic Relationship tied to a painful and traumatic past life that had ended badly. For seven years they had been in the Karmic Relationship revolving door, reliving some of the same dynamics from their previous lifetime together, but with unique challenges from this life added to the mix.

Kirsten's Soul Journeys session to the past life helped both her and Dave to diffuse their anger toward each other. Surprisingly when Kirsten told Dave about the past life, he accepted the validity of this experience. It had the ring of truth for him. Kirsten found this unusual because Dave typically denied taking responsibility for any of his hurtful or painful actions. In fact, he had a fear of his temper or the expression of any intense emotion. According to Kirsten, Dave would let his feelings build up like a pressure cooker and then he'd explode. Of course, his suppression of anger could have been a residue from the tragedy of their past life together. His deep-seated fear could also have been the Shadow that had formed in his psyche from having killed his wife. Without the opportunity to do a Soul Journey with Dave, I can't confirm this hypothesis. Nonetheless, it's very likely the couple had several past lives together.

past life present challenges

One of Dave's challenges in this life was to learn to let his feelings out gradually without fearing that his anger would be destructive, if he expressed it openly. His reaction to anger was understandable because of his unconscious memory of its destructive effect.

According to Kirsten, other present-life challenges for Dave were a fear of betrayal and an inability to give unconditional love to his love partner. Due to the past life when he had killed his wife out of jealousy, Dave carried into this lifetime a sense that she would be unfaithful to him. In fact, Kirsten's attractions to other men had been a factor in the couple's previous separations. Because the past-life experience had made Dave believe he could never trust his wife, he pushed her away emotionally. This set the stage for a self-fulfilling replay of their past-life Karmic Relationship and Shadow projections. In their case, history repeated itself again but in a less tragic manner.

Another challenge for Dave in their marriage was to be more flexible, warm, expressive, and accepting of his wife. This could only occur if he became less judgmental and more trusting. For this to happen, he would certainly need to feel a greater sense of love, devotion, and contentment from Kirsten.

Kirsten's challenges from their past life together were to balance her independent, assertive, and strong side with her passive, vulnerable, nurturing, and receptive side. Fearful of being hurt again, she'd never allowed herself to truly surrender and trust. This had led to her not being fully committed to their marriage.

If you recall, Kirsten had been extremely critical of very feminine women whom she saw as weak, passive, controlled, and sometimes victimized by their partners. Because of the trauma she suffered in her past life in such a role, these traits became a part of her Shadow or suppressed personality. This was the side of her mother she didn't like, and it made her angry to see her own Shadow displayed in other women.

As with her husband, Kirsten's primary test was to learn to trust. She needed the courage to honor her own self and feelings in the relationship and then trust her partner to respect them.

During her marriage to Dave, Kirsten often allowed herself to be controlled. This resulted in having her become the passive, dependent type of woman she so feared and despised. Kirsten lamented that she had become her mother during this marriage, and would reactively lurch from one extreme to the other. One day, she'd be dependent and the next day, rebellious. Her past-life traumas had resulted in an array of unresolved reactive patterns.

Kirsten also had other issues with her Karmic Relationship and Shadow projections that were tied to having been buried alive. Kirsten feared any expression of anger or physical aggression. If anyone tapped or pushed against her chest, she'd fly into a rage. She was so acutely sensitive to pressure on her chest and body that she would only sleep with lightweight blankets and had to fluff them up so that they only barely touched her body.

As you can see from this example, both Kirsten and Dave were alike—the like attracts like principle—in that they each needed to express more vulnerability. For their marriage to get out of the Karmic Relationship revolving door, Kirsten would have to surrender more to her soft feminine side, and Dave needed to display more emotion, feeling, and flexibility. For both of them, this meant acknowledging and accepting their Shadow selves. Kirsten, at least, had the opportunity to experience her Shadow directly and literally in a past-life Soul Journey. Once this was done, she could fully receive the gift of the Shadow. That gift is emotional balance and personal power.

past-life fear of pain or loss

As you can see, unconscious fear of pain and loss from past lives were the basis for Kirsten and Dave's marital problems in this life. The core challenge with Karmic Relationships of any type is the unconscious pain and fear of various flavors that souls carry forward into their next lifetimes.

As fate would have it, these realizations and my sessions with Kirsten came at the end of her marriage to Dave. Partially from our Soul Journey work together and the healings it evoked, Kirsten and Dave remained best friends in spite of getting divorced. They often support one another in life and with their subsequent love relationships by calling and occasionally visiting to see how things are going. They also appreciate each other more and have an understanding of the dynamics that shaped the difficulties in their marriage.

Armed with this insight, Kirsten and Dave are now able to be more responsive instead of reactive in their current love relationships. They no longer are doomed to repeat their karmic patterns of the past.

When you resolve traumas from past lives, you and the people with whom you have relationships can dissolve their fears. This means that they will no longer condition or cripple your thoughts and actions. You will both have the freedom to live fully in the present and not in the past. In Kirsten's case, her husband could support her past life recall because he intuitively recognized the truth of her experience. Even though I didn't work with Dave directly, both partners reaped the primary benefit of doing Soul Journeys to past lives. They gained the ability to live and love more fully in the present. This is karma and reincarnation in action.

Kirsten's attitudes toward receptive and feminine women also shifted. Instead of reacting to these traits within others and herself, she could now see their value and embrace those parts of herself. With this shift, the men she attracted did not have to be much stronger than her or exhibit signs of being too controlling and dominating. Nor did the men in her life need to carry or express her suppressed feminine side, which she'd always find initially appealing but would later view as a weakness.

Recognizing the roots of this type of relationship is the first step toward resolving the karma that drew two people together. Hopefully, some of the questions asked in the beginning, in which you might have had some doubt as to whether they related to you or not, are now clearer. In Chapter 11, when you go through the Soul Journeys process, you can focus on the Shadow Karmic Relationship you've identified to gain greater clarity about its karmic underpinnings and what it is mirroring for you today.

Now, in Chapter 5, we'll explore your most primary hidden wound. It festers in your psyche and secretly poisons your relationships. The fear wound forms the nest for all your other hidden wounds. Learning to identify and resolve invisible fear will allow you to express your highest ideals and release karmic energy that has bound you to souls and situations for eons.

part 2

recognizing your
invisible relationship wounds

chapter 5

The Fear Wound

THE VAST MAJORITY OF PEOPLE OPERATE AUTOMATICALLY, AS IF IN A dream or nightmare, driven by the emotional energy of fear. Some mistake fear for motivation. Others mislabel fear as common sense, claiming that it is only rational to avoid certain people, places, and things. Meanwhile, invisible Fear Wounds hold their negative behavioral patterns and life themes unconsciously in place.

All invisible wounds are basically Fear Wounds. Even though your wounds may have been caused by loss, betrayal, abandonment, or pain they all have at their core the four-letter word: *fear.* Sometimes I wonder if fear is the whip used against souls by the forces of darkness. Maybe fear is actually more like a fire used to temper a soul by burning away its seemingly unending desire for more power and control.

On an instinctual level we all seem to be hardwired to overcome fear with power, but we never have enough power to completely eradicate fear and bring a true sense of security. The quest for power becomes unending. The challenge is to transcend our human instinctual programming for survival via power and begin to recognize and apply the survival strategies of the soul or the spiritual self. Healing invisible Fear Wounds and other wounds that are buried in the unconscious moves us from the Credit and Debit Karmic Relationships, which are based on power, to the Soul Agreement and Beyond Karma Relationships, which are based on unconditional love.

Often after several sessions in which I've helped someone to resolve trauma from past lives, certain clients have asked if there is anything they did that was not motivated or influenced by past pain and fear. They are quick to understand that they have been confined by fear on all sides, much more effectively than they'd ever realized.

We all are.

In the next two stories, I will show you how Fear Wounds can show up in different ways. First, you will see an example in Anna's sessions of unhealed Anger Wounds from past lives and what they created. We discovered that these unaddressed wounds had set in place a fear response in her present life that led to people pleasing and physical ailments.

Anna, an intelligent, attractive, happily married woman in her 40s, came to my office for treatment. Her work involved worldwide travel and public presentations. Even though she was successful, Anna had always considered herself to be a *people pleaser.*

Anna constantly overcompensated in her work and relationships to keep from being the target for anyone's anger. Occasionally, the combined stress of her job and attempts to avoid confrontation resulted in severe migraine headaches with pain extending down her back and spine. Over the years, Anna had tried all types of treatments from over-the-counter medications to acupuncture, chiropractics, and meditation. Nothing had provided significant or lasting relief for her migraines.

Although Anna had learned to live with the tension in her neck and back, on the day she came to see me, she was having the beginnings of a painful migraine. As we began her Soul Journeys therapy, Anna sat stiffly. It was apparent she was having difficulty turning her head from side to side. I've often noticed that on the day of a Soul Journey past-life session my clients experience an emergence of symptoms related to the trauma they are about to relive. This is a result of the unconscious starting to bring out painful experiences that are ripe for release.

Here's how Anna's session unfolded:

Since I suspect that Anna is already experiencing trauma tied to a painful past life, I have her close her eyes and focus on her head and back pain. I cue her for the past life where the pain began. She immediately describes being in the aftermath of a brutal battle. When I ask her to tell me if she is male or female, she describes herself as a large, young male, with blonde hair. As Anna lies on my sofa, she is very animated, thrashing, and grimacing as if she's directly experiencing the scene she's viewing in her mind.

Anna finds herself viewing the aftermath of a battle during which she's a young Viking warrior who has been captured alive and taken as prisoner. It is late in the evening, and the prisoner is taken away from the battlefield to a nearby hut. They tie him facedown with rough rope, tear his clothes off his back, and brutally torture him. Several enemy soldiers participate in the abuse. They slowly taunt and beat him, as if for sport.

When torture experiences such as Anna's emerge, sessions can run longer than usual or may need to be continued in a following session. When I'm faced with resolving past-life torture experiences, I liken it to a surgeon opening a patient only to find infection that has spread much beyond the point of origin. It takes time, patience, and persistence to get the patient to discharge all the painful emotional remnants.

During Anna's Soul Journey session, she finally recalled the moment of death. The warrior's assailants systematically smash the back of his head and spinal column with a heavy wooden club. While Anna relives this brutal experience, she thrashes on the sofa in my office as she shouts out the words of fear, pain, and anger that rise up in her. We review the highlights of the trauma and death several times to ensure that all emotional attachments to it have been severed.

After Anna releases the emotions and memories of this past-life drama, she opens her eyes wide with amazement and nearly jumps up from my sofa. As she stretches and (moves her neck left to right), Anna begins to weep. For the first time in her adult life, Anna feels absolutely no head, back, or neck pain. She tells me that she can't recall when she could twist and turn without feeling stiffness and tension in her neck and back. She can feel that something has been released for the first time.

In addition to healing physical suffering, Anna gained insight from her Soul Journey to view the moment of death that had been affecting her life today. She realized her need to please and not anger others had stemmed from this past life, when her torturer's anger had resulted in a brutal death. After this session, Anna went on with her life, no longer fearful when people directed anger at her. She began to assert herself when her own needs were going unfulfilled. In a follow up with Anna, after approximately one year, I found that she had remained free of migraines and the chronic stiffness in her neck and back. Pleasing others or fear of their anger, she quite literally viewed to be a thing of the past.

For story number two, I will share an experience while lecturing, training, and doing Soul Journeys work in Brazil. This will give an example of how sometimes we can generate seemingly irrational fears from past-life experiences that show up in present lives.

A psychologist brought her 10-year-old son Benito to me for treatment. Benito had always had an irrational fear of needles or any sharp objects. He was so sensitized to this that even knitting needles would send him quickly out of the room where they were being used.

His mother had grown increasingly concerned because as Benito grew older receiving a shot for medical purposes had become nearly impossible due to his fear. She could recall no developmental explanation from childhood for his extreme fear of needles or sharp objects so she took the opportunity to bring him to me for help.

Benito's mother, a Brazilian, was married to a Japanese businessman then living in Japan. During the marriage they had only lived in Brazil and the son had not been exposed to the Japanese language, and the couple communicated only in Portuguese. Now divorced, Benito had recently spent a summer in Japan with his father and curiously had learned to read and speak fluent Japanese in only three months. His parents had been amazed at this and were at a loss to explain it.

When I first saw Benito, he was very cooperative and respectful. I spent a little time talking with him to establish rapport. I asked him about his visit to Japan and he quickly told me that he much preferred Japan to Brazil and wanted to live there. He was not unhappy with his mother and family in Brazil, but just liked Japan better. I casually asked him about his fear of needles or sharp objects and he said that they just made him uncomfortable.

With Benito, I decided to focus directly on the past life causing his fear and avoid exposing him to a museum full of past-life images as is sometimes done with adults. When he lay down on the sofa and closed his eyes, he immediately found himself kneeling by a stream cupping his hands in a river to get a drink of water. In this past life he was a Japanese male with a bow and quiver of arrows on his back wearing a military uniform. His horse waited nearby as he took in the beauty of the forest. A battle had recently ended and he and his fighters had been victorious in defeating the enemy.

As he kneeled by the stream, I was intrigued at how this 10-year-old boy described the lilting flight of a leaf he noticed falling from a tree and slowly landing in the stream in front of him. It was poetic in a Zen manner of speaking. It was apparent he was in a Japanese mindset as he relived this event.

After drinking his fill, he stood up to take in the calm of the forest before mounting his horse. Suddenly there was a quick hissing sound and a thud. He looked down and to his shock, saw that an arrowhead was sticking out the front of his chest. He had been shot through the heart. He struggled to remove the arrow but found it impossible, and crumpled to the ground dying.

After we resolved the trauma of his death I brought him back to present time and he sat up. Benito didn't seem at all surprised at what he had experienced and after a brief discussion we ended the session. His mother and I spoke and I explained to her what had happened and asked her to find an opportunity within the next several days to see if his fear still remained. The very next day she called me with an interesting report.

Earlier that day, she had been sitting in a room where she had sewing equipment and called to Benito. When he came in she casually handed him a pincushion full of pins and needles. She said that ordinarily he would not even take such a cushion and would fearfully leave the room at the site of it. On this occasion, he calmly took the cushion and even removed one of the pins and slowly examined it. After a minute or two he replaced the pin and set the cushion down. He displayed no fear or apprehension at all for the first time in his life. Her call was to confirm that the session with him the previous day had been successful at releasing his fear of sharp pointed objects.

Of course his Japanese past life also explained his affinity for Japan and the ease at which he learned to read and speak the language during the summer stay with his dad. This is one of the many ways Soul Journeys into past lives can explain and resolve seemingly irrational fears. I've often said that the irrational often becomes very rational when you consider past lives.

fear comes with the territory

My experience suggests that each soul has felt fear from the first day it incarnated here on this planet. Just the very fact of arriving from heaven into this strange and unknown realm probably elicited fear. From that point on it was all about struggle. Throughout your many lifetimes, pain and fear continued to be interspersed with brief periods of joy, pleasure, and contentment. You may already be familiar with how invisible Fear Wounds form a pattern in your life today. It may also be the case that just when things are really going great, you begin to wonder, or fear, when the other shoe will drop.

The question is, why does this happen?

On an instinctual level fear certainly had its survival value in the dawn of human awareness and continues to fulfill a function of alerting you when you're facing an emergency situation. We live in a world of duality going through positive and negative experiences, creation, and destruction. Life on earth includes the experience of pain. Fear is the offspring of pain.

When a soul incarnates on this planet the first time and during it's many subsequent incarnations, it experiences pain and fear of attack, disease, accidents, and loss. That pain plants seeds of fear in the unconscious. Once deeply rooted, those ancient seeds of fear grow and expand until they're affecting more and more of your present day thoughts, words, and actions.

Next thing you know, karmic patterns and life themes are in place, and the drama and trauma of life is in full swing. Eventually you recognize the strategies you've been using for gaining control while you were futilely attempting to avoid pain and fear. You begin to wonder if there is a way you could get off of the fear treadmill. That wake-up call, alerting you to the possibility of healing your invisible Fear Wounds, comes from the soul. It is asking your tired and weary human self if you're ready to find a better way; a way to truly embrace love and move beyond fear. That day, when you hear the call of soul, heralds your true spiritual awakening.

Awakening suggests the beginning of a newly found freedom. Its possibility has remained unknown while you were under the thumb of illusion that only karmic law rules.

The soul now whispers through the din of your fear-burdened lifetimes, awakening you to the law of love. Even your Karmic Relationships start and continue because there is something about love that you still need to learn.

For me, my grandmother was an example of the law of love in action. I recall years ago at her funeral, the minister's eulogy spoke words about her deeds and accomplishments. But I found it obvious that all of my grandmother's achievements were far overshadowed by the many things she did as an expression of love. Her loving acts touched the lives of others in large and seemingly small ways.

If you could attend your own funeral and write your eulogy, what would you want said about the way you have lived your life? Give it a try. In the end, what will those you have left behind believe was most important to you? Are you willing to live now the way you'd like to be remembered? Do you yearn to begin healing the unconscious fears that keep you from fully realizing the law of love in your life? Discovering, dissolving, and becoming free of invisible Fear Wounds will transform you into the kind of loving and courageous person you've always wanted to be.

fear of poverty

It's surprising to me how many successful, accomplished, and driven people that come to me have had a subconscious fear of being destitute or homeless. Part of my goal in these situations is to help dissolve their fear of extreme poverty. Then they can embrace the joy and love in life, in their accomplishments, and in their relationships.

With the thousands of lifetimes we've all experienced, you have to assume everyone has had the destitute/homeless experience in some past life or another. The devastating effects of those lives are not only in proportion to what you experienced while being destitute and homeless. The level of intensity with which pain or fear still poisons your unconscious is also determined by the acute emotional trauma you've experienced under dire circumstances.

For years, you've heard sayings and seen titles such as, "There is nothing to fear but fear itself," or "Feel the fear but do it anyway." This is easy to say and an obvious truth. But how do you override fear, when most are conditioned to operate in *Fear Everything And Run?*

When you are in the throes of fear, you are in the throes of fear.

Your reaction to whatever you fear is automatic and largely unconscious. Even when you become aware that you are fearful, how do you go through, around, or suppress such an emotion and "be wonderful," as a friend of mine is so fond of saying? The plain and simple answer is that you can't.

Until you uncover and discharge the energy locked within the unconscious causing your fears, you can kiss any real freedom of choice and self-determination good-bye. Invisible Fear Wounds will make you *be* the effect of your relationships and environment, instead of the cause.

And you will find it is impossible to feel or give unconditional love in the midst of fear. What invisible Fear Wounds are holding you back from the promise and fulfillment of unconditional love?

fear of success

What if you came to my office and said that you seemed to have a fear of success? You lament that whenever you're on the verge of making financial dreams a reality, you do something to bring it all to an end. This was the case with Lisa.

Lisa is an attractive 35-year-old blonde with two younger sisters. She loves horses, dogs, and all animals and has owned horses in the past. Years earlier, she had been a barrel racer and competitive team roper in rodeos. Needless to say, she knew horses well. Currently her animal companion is an Australian sheepdog. The mere thought of losing him brings tears to her eyes.

Lisa has a natural knack for business and is self-employed with a growing service that involves working with divorce attorneys. When she first came to me, Lisa had just purchased a Porsche and started a relationship with a new boyfriend. She mentioned that most of her relationships had been brief although she would love to have a long-term partnership.

Lisa identified her greatest problem as a possible unconscious fear of success. Try as she might to sustain momentum, she continually seemed to sabotage herself when success seemed imminent.

At crucial times in her life, Lisa would not pay bills on time even though she had the funds. This would later cause credit problems that could have been easily avoided. At other times, she diverted important funds for expenses related to her hobby of riding and roping in rodeos. Until recently, she had to delay starting the business that she had contemplated doing for years.

During the time when her plans were on hold, Lisa chose to work for unreasonable attorneys who made her life difficult, at best. She often found that she knew her specialty better than they did, but was not allowed to work in a way that would most benefit either them or her. This resulted in Lisa often switching jobs from one attorney to the next and never gaining much momentum toward fulfilling the dream of beginning her own business.

The first past life Lisa experienced in her Soul Journey brought to the surface her fear of success.

At the very beginning of our session, Lisa found herself in an incarnation when she had been a male in Europe during the 1800s. She observed a man in his mid-50s walking down a cobblestone street after a business meeting. He wore a hat with a feather quill, velvet knickers, suede leather shoes with pointy ends, and a puffy-sleeved shirt. An unattractive man, he was overweight with a large belly.

Although early evening, it was dark outside and had rained, making the air a little damp. As the man passed a familiar area of the city, he noticed tall, three-story houses along the street. He approached a tunnel, which was cut into the hillside, and began to walk through it, whistling as he looked around. When he emerged at the other end of the tunnel, more houses were spread out along the street and large trees grew on the right side of the avenue.

The man crossed a small bridge and finally arrived at his own two-story house where he lived with his wife and children. A breeder and Thoroughbred racer, the man kept his horses in the stables beside this house. He was very successful at his business and had a sizable staff of trainers, jockeys, and helpers who lived or worked on his estate.

On this evening when the man returned home, the fireplace crackled, and the maid greeted him, taking his coat and hat. Before settling down for the evening, he heard a noise outside the house. Curious, he pushed the big iron rings, which opened two heavy wooden front doors, and walked into the courtyard. There, he saw three men approaching. "What do these men need?" he wondered.

The men didn't look respectable. As they drew closer, he noticed their bad teeth. Even though these were strangers, he was unafraid and politely asked, "How can I help you?"

The stranger in the forefront said with a smirk, "We don't need your help." Then he quickly pulled out from his pocket a long, pointed dagger and thrust it into the left side of the man's stomach.

The man immediately collapsed. Lying on the courtyard cobblestones, bleeding and mortally wounded, he suddenly realized that these strangers were some of his competitors in the horse industry. They had wanted to force him out of the business. He had become almost unbeatable because his trainers, jockeys, and Thoroughbreds were so good.

As the man died, he reflected on the good life he'd had with his wife and children. In addition, he felt that he was going to miss smoking his cigars and pipes, his home, and his beloved horses. Eventually someone came out and found his lifeless body. For a while, as soul, he hovered above the physical body he'd just left. He watched his wife bending over him and crying as the servants ran out of the house. He sadly thought, "This was a good life."

After her Soul Journeys session Lisa could clearly see why she committed acts of self-sabotage whenever she became successful. She had a big "Ah-ha" realization when she figured out that to her unconscious mind, financial success, marriage, and a family had become associated with pain, death, and loss. She'd even had horses at various times in her current life but was unable to keep them, causing history to repeat itself again, although on a smaller scale.

hidden fears dictate new choices

Later, Lisa had a memory of another life she had lived right after the one in which she'd been a successful horse trainer and racer.

In this next life she recalled being a middle-aged white male who was around 6'3" tall. Fairly attractive, he was the strong and rugged type with weathered skin and a clean-shaven face. Lisa described the man as having big hands and squinty eyes from working long hours in the sun. He wore a straw cowboy hat, jeans, and a long-sleeved cotton shirt.

This man lived in a sparsely populated area of the Australian outback. He avoided any significant love relationships or business activities and lived only with his Australian sheepdog. His closest friend was a neighbor far down the road.

The Aussie man would go into town from time to time to get supplies, drink alcohol, and meet women in the saloon but he never married. He died when his horse got spooked by a rattler and reared, throwing him off the back. The man hit his head on a rock and died alone with only his horse standing over him.

fear lived on

A common positive theme in those two past lives, which carried over into Lisa's present-life, was her need for and ability to have close relationships with animals, specifically dogs and horses. On the negative side, Lisa's hidden fears and their effect on her ability to succeed are examples of how unconscious and invisible wounds, stemming from past lives, influence the present-life. Her past life as a man, who died because his jealous competitors perceived him as too successful, led to the lifetime in which he was an Australian loner, who cut himself off from relationships and any semblance of a successful life. In her current lifetime, Lisa, burdened with invisible fear, had been depriving herself of the success that should rightfully come from her natural business sense and positive work habits.

It so happened that Lisa came to see me at a time when she had finally started her dream business, and it was going well. Recognizing her life pattern of self-sabotage, she came to realize that if it had gone unresolved she would unconsciously replay it again in her life. Our sessions together gave Lisa the release she needed to let go of her fear of success and move forward with greater confidence and objectivity.

As with Lisa's experiences, on the surface, your life may seem to be unfolding as the result of a logical flow of events and circumstances, but karmic energy is actually rolling underneath and directing the drama. Releasing karmic energy, which has been locking pain and fear in the unconscious, opens infinite possibilities of experience. This gives you greater freedom to escape your prison of fear and choose and create your own destiny.

At the opposite end of the love spectrum is fear. The law of karma is expressed through the use or abuse of power. The more power you exert, even if it's in order to survive, the more karma you generate. This cycle becomes an endless loop that keeps you in a hypnotic grip for eons of time.

Finally, you must confront what every advanced soul eventually has to face: No matter how powerful you become, love is the only true way out of your karmic prisons. Power and fear will keep you trapped and incarnating in and out of one Karmic Relationship after another.

uncovering invisible fear wounds

Invisible Fear Wounds poison and inhibit your thoughts, words, and actions in ways you may not recognize. Use the survey below to decide if you have hidden Fear Wounds that may be holding you back from expressing yourself fully, freely, and positively in relationships.

You'll refer to the findings of this survey when you have the Soul Journeys experience I'll describe in Chapter 11.

- Are there scenes on TV or in movies that you avoid watching or feel extreme discomfort at the sight of?

- Do you avoid certain people, places, or groups because of the anxiety that you feel in their presence?

- Is there someone in your past that has done something that you've been unable to forgive?

- Do you have an exaggerated emotional reaction to an event, place, or action with no rational basis or explanation for why you react to it?

- Is there anywhere on your body where you cannot tolerate being touched, held, or restrained?

- Do you have recurrent dreams or nightmares that force you awake and leave you shaken or upset?

- Do you often have thoughts of losing someone close to you that make you feel extremely anxious and upset?

If you answered "yes" to any of these questions, you're very likely carrying invisible Fear Wounds from your past. Certainly there may be an explanation for manifestations of fear based on your known present-life experiences, but very often your reactions, as indicated by the answers to this survey, indicate that the problems you're experiencing in relationships have much deeper roots in past-life or pre-birth traumas.

In the next chapter, you'll discover if fear's children—the twin traumas of abandonment and loss—are trapping you in damaging or disappointing relationships.

chapter 6

The Abandonment and Loss Wounds

DEEP DOWN, ALL PEOPLE DESIRE UNION OR BONDING WITH OTHERS. BUT to have depth or substance, true love in relationships requires a certain amount of vulnerability—an emotional willingness to trust and expose our hearts to the opportunity for joy and fulfillment and at times, the pain of life. Yet we're often unable to embrace true intimacy. Unless we release ourselves to heart vulnerability, relationships don't run deep and are impermanent without flowering into true and sustaining bonds of love.

Since so many of us have the pervasive drive for union in relationships, this suggests a universal desire that is transcendent and spawned from a deep inner source. Often, the desire for a close relationship emerges as a romantic drive to pursue a so-called soul mate—that perfect other half. For some, searching for a soul mate becomes an obsessive preoccupation. The source of such a drive for union arises from that divine spark of the Absolute that resides within us all. Questing for union with the Absolute, which for most is unconscious, creates a never-ending thirst that gets expressed and distorted by all manner of relationships, desires, and ambitions. These drives often manifest as pursuit of dominance, power, control, recognition, pleasure, and any of the addictions in life. In other words, without realizing it, people are looking for God in all the wrong places.

A certain Chassidic story comes to mind here.

A Hasid complained to a Rabbi that certain people were turning night into day by playing cards until the sun rises and sleeping till the sun sets.

"That is good," said the zaddik. Like all the people, card-players want to serve God and don't know how. But this way, they are learning to stay awake and persist in doing something. When they have become perfect in their wakefulness, all they need to do is turn to God. What excellent servants they will make for Him then!"

hidden wounds sabotage vulnerability

Past Abandonment and Loss Wounds, which are actually expressions of the Fear Wound, frequently hide behind a person's inability to allow true heart vulnerability. More than any other I've observed from facilitating Soul Journeys, Abandonment and Loss Wounds have a dimension that impacts your relationship with God, religion, or the spirit within.

Many of you have come into this life with seeds of abandonment and loss that are easily reactivated by the defeats you've experienced in this lifetime or your early-life losses, such as the separation and divorce of your parents when you were only a child. Perhaps, Abandonment and Loss Wounds resurfaced and became a factor that lingered in your life when you felt alienation from friends or playmates. The sudden death of someone close or the heartbreak of having to end a love relationship or deep friendship may also have activated deeper Abandonment and Loss Wounds. Sometimes, the life theme of having Abandonment and Loss as your invisible wounds can be triggered by merely the thought of or imagining that you have been abandoned by someone close to you.

Possessiveness, jealousy, codependency, insecurity, fear of intimacy, or the feeling that you are all alone, even when you're with others, are common effects tied to Abandonment and Loss Wounds.

getting to the deep roots of invisible wounds

Present-life experience seems to mirror more fundamental and damaging past-life history. For this reason, it's often necessary to return to the primary source in past lives to heal invisible wounds.

This was the case of Charlotte, who was in her late 40s when she first came to see me. An attractive blonde with short hair and of medium height, she was neatly dressed, almost business-like, with tan pants and matching tunic jacket over a white sweater. Her friendly and engaging manner suggested a certain interpersonal ease and comfort. During our intake interview, Charlotte voiced no specific complaints but did say she had several issues that affected her relationships with others. Right away, I could see she had a tendency to downplay the significance of her own problems.

A warm and open person, Charlotte is the Human Resources director for a small company that manufactures and distributes a specialized product. Her boss referred to Charlotte as the glue that holds the company and staff/employees together. Her warm personality made her effective, even with those in the company with whom she'd had difficult exchanges. Charlotte had an excellent reputation for being able to successfully orchestrate people and get things done. My perception of Charlotte was that she could find the silver lining in any cloud. Part of the reason she didn't have specific complaints until now, was that she'd been unwilling to commit to much of anything, including healing her own hidden wounds. But Charlotte had attended one of my workshops and after listening to me speak about invisible wounds and Karmic Relationships, she wanted to follow up by having a personal Soul Journeys session. After the first half-hour in my office, I could clearly see that Charlotte had been suppressing deep emotional wounds. However, her initial interest in seeing me suggested more of a casual curiosity in exploring her past lives.

I soon concluded that Charlotte's perpetual optimism masked a difficult and painful childhood. When she was between the ages of five and seven, her dad was in two major auto accidents that had nearly killed him. While she was still a little girl, he had left her mom, whom she described as "crazy." Her mother had been committed to psychiatric institutions twice during the course of Charlotte's life and had received electroconvulsive or shock therapy.

Charlotte went to a Catholic school and had two sisters, one of whom was adopted. She mentioned some family secret around this adoption that no one would discuss. Born with a clubfoot, Charlotte wore a cast for years during her childhood.

By the way, Charlotte also revealed that, when she was five years old, an uncle had sexually molested her. Years later, when she'd mentioned the molestation, her mother responded by telling Charlotte that she herself had been molested as a child. She advised her daughter that there was no need to make a big deal over such an experience.

well-hidden wounds

As you can see, Charlotte had experienced challenge after challenge while growing up, but none of the effects of these hurtful events were apparent when anyone casually interacted with her. She was one of those strong, cheerful types whom everyone else brought his or her problems to.

Charlotte felt bothered by two primary issues that she quietly seemed unable to resolve or manage within herself. First, she reported having trouble bonding with and keeping people in her life. She recognized that something within her maintained a certain distance from others. Her relationships were transient and lacked depth. She felt this lack of intimate connection had been a factor in her previous marriages.

Charlotte's second big concern was that she was terrified of her younger brother. While they were growing up, he had been quite volatile. She'd spent most of her childhood trying to avoid being alone with him. This fear started at such a young age that she couldn't remember when she didn't feel it. As a grown woman, she still experienced terror in her relationship with him. Now, her brother had a terminal illness, but Charlotte was having great difficulty reaching out to him, even though he wasn't expected to live more than another year.

Since attending my workshop, a man Charlotte was in love with and had been seeing for the past seven years had suddenly died of a heart attack. Earlier, on the evening of his death, the couple had gone out for a romantic dinner in a nearby restaurant. Later, as they lay in bed at home after lovemaking, her lover had died tragically in Charlotte's arms.

They had a constant on-and-off relationship, because Charlotte's boyfriend had been fearful of completely letting go and embracing their deep bond. His reticence had especially caused pain, because this was the only relationship Charlotte had ever been willing to embrace wholeheartedly. She tried to break off with him many times, feeling that it was better for their relationship to be either all or nothing. However, whenever she tried to bring about a separation, this boyfriend's life and business would go downhill, and Charlotte would feel compelled to be there for him.

Since her boyfriend's death, Charlotte had started to feel that there was no real reason for her to go on living. Even though she was clear that suicide wasn't an option for her, she still felt at a loss to find any desire to continue her life. She had few close friends or attachments and in her words, "I'm not passionate about anything. I love but not too much; and I hate but not too much."

Charlotte's friends experienced her as such a cheerful optimist that she felt she could never open up and share with them her lack of enthusiasm for life and living.

As is often the case, Charlotte had a cluster of issues that seemed to adversely influence her life and relationships. With the sudden death of the man she loved, she understandably felt much grief, but curiously it did not show in her outward persona. Her warm, engaging demeanor remained in spite of the pain she felt within her heart. She could not even allow herself to openly and truly grieve.

a relationship role reversal

After gathering details of Charlotte's life history, I initiated a Soul Journeys session to identify the roots of her cycle of pain and distance in relationships.

A key lifetime found her as a young, male warrior in England during the Middle Ages. We entered the scene during a battle in which the warrior fought against adversaries, back-to-back, along with 20 to 30 other men. With swords drawn, the enemy swarmed the grounds and rode the hilly, open county on horseback toward the warriors. A comrade named Garth, an older man, fought nearby. He had been like a father to the young warrior, raising him since his early teen years.

Suddenly, in the heat of battle, the young warrior noticed a man on horseback angling for Garth's back. In an effort to prevent a fatal assault of his friend, the warrior dashed between the man and Garth and couldn't avoid taking a sword in the chest. Garth turned, saw what had happened, and took the attacker out with his own sword. Garth then dropped down on a knee and held his younger comrade up in his arms as the warrior lay on the ground, fatally wounded.

The battle raged on while the young comrade told Garth to let him die and save himself. Garth promised that he wouldn't leave his friend. He finally succeeded in carrying him to shelter in a nearby stable.

Garth watched helplessly as his friend lay dying. He blamed himself for allowing this tragedy to happen. His dying friend and comrade assured Garth that he wasn't responsible and that he would have attempted to save him again, if he'd had the chance. Before taking his last breath, the young warrior finally said that this had been a life well lived.

During her past-life Soul Journey, Charlotte instantly recognized Garth as her reincarnated love partner of this lifetime. After she resolved the emotional trauma of being the young warrior who had died tragically in Garth's arms, Charlotte understood that in her current life, the roles were reversed. This time, it had been she who held the loved one, dying in her arms. Charlotte now understood why she'd found it so difficult to once again accept saying good-bye to and losing this person/soul she had loved and lost not once but twice.

abandonment and loss, once again

In her next Soul Journeys session, Charlotte discovered that she'd not only been involved with this same soul, who had been Garth in the Middle Ages and her lover in the current life, but their paths had crossed yet another time.

This Soul Journeys process brought Charlotte into a pre-Civil War scene. It began with Charlotte seeing herself as a 16-year-old girl riding in a carriage one day with her father, Paul, in Charleston, South Carolina. Her name was Annabelle. She was a slender girl with blonde hair, blue eyes, and fair skin. Annabelle, an only child, and her father, a businessman, had a happy relationship. Due to the loss of Annabelle's mother when she was a little girl, the father and daughter had become especially close. They lived a protected and safe life in a large Southern home where the child was taken care of well.

When Annabelle turned 18, she fell in love with and married John, one of her father's business associates. John was around thirty five years old at the time, and her father did not fully approve of their marriage.

The newly married couple lived in a two-story colonial house with columns in the front. As time went on, Annabelle gave birth to two boys. John, who owned a shipping business, had become involved in an unsafe deal. This affair greatly displeased Annabelle's father, but both her father and husband kept Annabelle in the dark about any specifics of the business arrangement.

One day, while Annabelle sat on the front porch, her father came to the house. He held Annabelle's hands and told her that John had been killed. Annabelle screamed and passed out. The servants immediately took her to an upstairs bedroom.

When Annabelle returned to consciousness, she saw her dad standing at the foot of the bed. At first, she asked him what had happened and then remembered what he had told her before she'd fainted. She screamed, "It can't be true! Tell me it's not true!"

Her father sat next to her, holding her hand and saying, "Belle, I'm sorry."

From this point on, Annabelle's life took a downturn. Heartbroken, she withdrew into her grief and stopped caring for herself or anyone else. Her father became angry because she would not eat, sleep, or care for her two young sons. She lost the will to live and finally got very sick.

One day, in 1857, Annabelle lay in bed while her father and two sons were in the room. She told her father that staying alive had just become too hard. She asked him to forgive her and to take care of her boys. She said that she loved them all then died while her boys and father watched and wept.

healing the invisible wounds

In this past life, Charlotte again had become tragically parted from a man she held dear. Her husband in the Civil War era lifetime was the same soul who had died of a heart attack in this life and had been her friend, Garth, in a previous lifetime. Upon reflection Charlotte also realized that the experience of losing her children during the life and death as Annabelle was the reason she hadn't wanted to have any kids in this life. It hurt too much to lose them. She concluded that reluctance to get close in any lasting way to anyone in this lifetime had been directly related to the pain of loss and abandonment in those past lives.

After our sessions Charlotte's sense of hopelessness and depression lifted. She was once again able to experience fulfillment in her life and work and to also accept the possibility of having another loving relationship with a man. In her case, although she would not have considered suicide, she would likely have continued to slip into a depression and apathy similar to that of her past life as Annabelle.

This is one of the many instances where loss or abandonment wounds from past lives, left unresolved, resulted in fear of intimacy, self-sabotage, and self-destructive patterns that had become nearly impossible to dissolve. Charlotte's tragic losses in this life had been acting as triggers to bring old feelings to the surface, front and center.

Certainly Charlotte had plenty of traumatic and tragic experiences from this life to draw from. However, these were merely the tip of the iceberg with the past-life traumas being more deeply wounding and damaging. These past lives also set the stage for what happened in her current life. Like unwanted weeds in a garden, pulling up their roots was necessary to fully remove them and clear the garden.

Do You Have Hidden Abandonment and Loss Wounds?

- Do you feel it's safer not to risk opening your heart to anyone and prefer to remain unattached emotionally?

- Do you find yourself sabotaging potentially fulfilling relationships before they get too serious?

- Do you find a reason to end a relationship if there is any hint that your partner has or may have a problem with you?

- Is it difficult for you to give up control in the relationship and surrender important decisions to your partner?

- Do you feel fear or anxiety when your partner leaves for a trip or during times when you don't know or are unsure where he or she is?

- Do you easily experience strong but unwarranted feelings of jealousy, suspicion, or insecurity with interactions between your partner and a member or members of the opposite sex?

- Do movies where there is an unexpected rejection or loss of a loved one cause you great sadness and upset, even though the movie doesn't remind you of anything that has happened in your current life?

If you answered "yes" to four of the seven questions above, then you likely have hidden Abandonment or Loss Wounds active from this and past lives. Recognizing the presence of these wounds is half the battle toward being able to heal them.

The following is an exercise you can use to help you notice and accept feelings of abandonment and loss the next time they are triggered. Doing the steps of this exercise will allow you to experience the full impact of your feelings without blame or denial.

First, take time out to journal the circumstance of your abandonment and loss feelings by writing your response and impressions about them. Next, before going to bed at night, ask the spirit within for a dream to clarify the true source of your feelings. During the night or the next morning, journal whatever you experience in your dreams that even hints at feelings of abandonment or loss. If you don't recall any dreams the first night, continue with your dream request. It may take several days. Review your dreams again approximately one week later for their deeper significance. You may also want to share the dream with a close and trusted friend and ask if your friend has further insight about it.

Our next chapter will bring us face-to-face with the invisible Anger Wound that may be poisoning the relationships in your life. This wound often goes unrecognized because those who carry it are sometimes in positions of power and recognition. Their spouses, partners, family members, or co-workers tiptoe around and accommodate those who have Anger Wounds. Undetected, Anger Wounds breed resentment in others and keep you from recognizing how much love you have and want to give.

chapter 7

The Anger Wound

THE KARMIC DYNAMIC EXPRESSED BY THOSE, WHO ARE DRIVEN BY ANGER, is the old adage, *Live by the sword. Die by the sword.*

In some, anger is like an opiate for the psyche. It can motivate by giving a false sense of power, control, or security. Anger dulls your sensitivity to discomfort or pain. People very often use anger to intimidate and manipulate others. It can even drive people to achieve a measure of success, but there is a price.

Like all the other hidden wounds, the Anger Wound falls under the umbrella of fear. The Fear Wound has two polarities of expression—fight and flight. Anger is the fight expression of fear.

At a primal level, both the fight and flight polarities of the Fear Wound are ego survival or self-preservation modes. This means if a snarling dog or boss threatens you, the behavior is unconsciously recognized as a threat based on cues from past experience. The ego, as your sense of self-preservation, then engages in a reaction involving either approach-and-defend (fight) or withdraw-and-avoid (flight). This process is purely mechanical, or digital, in nature, and even the choice you make is based on past success or failure with fight or flight.

You can tell what your mode for responding to anger/fear is by looking back on how you've handled it in the past. For instance, when someone says or does something undesirable or threatening, whether intentional or not, do you lash out in reaction and fight or fearfully retreat and take flight?

Even though these responses are mechanical or reactive, you may be able to get by with their use, but both fight and flight have limited effectiveness. They are activated unconsciously and based on previous experiences of pain and defeat.

When I was a teenager being trained in the martial arts, my Sensei would emphasize that the best defense, when physically confronted, was to calm your reaction and if possible, just walk away from a fight or threat. To some this could be seen as flight, but the difference is the conscious choice based on understanding or even compassion instead of fear.

Let's look at an old samurai story for a moment:

Once upon a time, a ronin (independent or mercenary) samurai attacked and killed a famous Shogun in spite of security and his personal samurai guard.

The ronin escaped without capture after the assassination. For years afterward, the personal guard of the murdered Shogun hunted the ronin from village to village. His task was to bring justice by avenging the murder of his beloved Shogun. It was his duty to do so as dictated by the code of Bushido.

However, the cunning ronin proved elusive and always stayed one step ahead of his pursuer. After many years of pursuit the loyal guard caught up to the ronin who was standing near a village vendor. He approached him from behind. He quickly drew his sword and demanded that the ronin turn and prepare to die.

The ronin turned slowly, but instead of drawing his sword in defense, he spit in the face of his adversary. The guard, caught by surprise by such an affront flinched, slowly sheathed his sword, and then withdrew never to return.

When later asked why after so many years of pursuit he simply let the ronin go free, he said that when the ronin spit in his face, the attack suddenly became personal. At that point, he could no longer serve as an impersonal instrument of retribution and would have violated the warrior code and ethic by attacking.

In other words, he got personally angry and would have killed in revenge. In so doing he would be karmicly bound to his victim resulting in another likely unpleasant encounter with this soul in a future life.

Following this along to present time, it could be that the ronin today is a surgeon. During an operation he makes a surgical mistake resulting in his patient's death who happens to be the past life samurai's father today. The samurai in turn takes the matter to court in his grief and anger, continuing the cycle. As you can see these karmic battles rage daily in thousands of ways even in our modern society.

The anger/fight expression of the fear polarity has gained more acceptance than flight in most cultures. In some societies, it is seen as more heroic to stand one's ground and confront or challenge an adversary than it is to withdraw. An Islamic saying reinforces this view by stating that, "A moment of cowardice can result in a lifetime of shame." Unfortunately, the threat of cowardice based on religious or political beliefs can drive us to shameful acts of aggression. The Anger Wound we see most vividly played out today is in acts of terrorism.

This form of aggression, whether done individually or as a group, always carries a price karmicly. It perpetuates the cycle of cause and effect that will eventually swing back upon the person or group it represents. A true understanding of, or appreciation for this principle is largely lost in today's global culture. National loss and outrage notwithstanding, political leaders and military personnel might find such an understanding instructive in the spirit with which we conduct military operations.

This is not to suggest that if attacked or threatened that one should ignore or accept abuse unchallenged. The question is how do we defend ourselves or take necessary aggressive action without incurring additional individual or group karma by our actions?

creativity versus hidden anger wounds

Higher up on the survival scale, the spiritual self or soul, becomes creative. This means that in the face of a threat or challenge, the soul adapts a creative response in the moment. It's like a jazz musician improvising on a song that is being played live. Because of the musician's ability to improvise, the song evolves into a new creative expression each time it's played. From moment to moment when life becomes a free-flowing liquid expression, we are no longer governed by knee-jerk emotional responses. Instead, we live the creative dance.

Let's look at the difference between a creative response and reactive anger by using the familiar and mundane example of being stopped for a speeding ticket. Often you may find yourself vacillating between anger and fear at the sight of flashing lights behind your car and the amplified voice of a police officer demanding that you pull over. When the officer walks over to your car, you may react angrily or fearfully and make excuses about why you were or were not speeding or in violation of traffic law. This is a very mechanical and primal fear response to the threat of authority either from experiences in this lifetime, a past lifetime, or both. Your angry reaction may also be compounded by the inconvenience of delay and the expense of a ticket. Such anger or excuses routinely result in your getting a ticket, as your anger causes the officer to be more determined than ever to make you pay. Since like attracts like, your anger will likely constellate anger in the officer and possibly make matters worse.

I'll admit I enjoy driving fast. As an adult over the years, the few times I've been stopped for speeding, I made the conscious choice to greet the officer kindly and honestly. Sometimes I've even used humor to poke fun at myself for speeding. In these situations the officer has responded with understanding and frequently has forgiven the need to write a ticket, deciding instead to only give me a warning.

This may not seem significant, but consider that in my situation I am talking about an African American male, and most often, white police officers. With today's heightened vigilance, as unfortunate as it may be, the odds are strongly against the outcome I've had in the past. Yet my example of having a police officer brush off the traffic violation shows how using the principle of heart-centered creative action is superior to having a reactive fight or flight expression that arises out of an unconscious Anger Wound. This is only one of the many ways that moving completely out of the anger bandwidth of emotional reactiveness has its advantages.

healing the anger wound in relationships

The same principle of creative action applies to relationships. A love relationship of my own comes to mind.

A woman, whom I dated shared with me her feeling of gratitude at being able to speak about anything going on between us without having me defensively react by trying to make her wrong or by making excuses about how my busy schedule was causing me problems. In her previous two relationships, when this woman had openly shared her feelings and concerns, she received blame or defensive responses, which she found to be hurtful to her and the relationship. With her previous companions, she'd never felt heard or accepted during exchanges that involved conflict and would feel that she'd been put on the defensive. It was surprising and refreshing to her when she found that I openly heard and accepted her feelings about issues such as wanting more quality time together or more advance planning for our dates. Hers seemed like a minor concern to me, but these types of issues with past boyfriends' responses had triggered fight or flight reactions in her. A reactive hidden Anger Wound had resulted in such arguments making her suppress her feelings and withdraw from the relationship or impulsively argue with the boyfriend.

On the occasions when she found it necessary to share her feelings regarding challenges in our relationship, I could see her quietly preparing herself to bring up a grievance. Once she did, we were both surprised at how much needless reluctance she had before speaking.

Sometimes old Anger Wounds go deep and result in fear and inhibition. Yet because I didn't have an automatic fight or flight reaction response to her concerns and could instead, offer the creative action of truly listening to her, she became able to express herself more freely and openly.

With any relationship getting beyond the need to react and allowing yourself to honestly, compassionately, and creatively respond to a situation is the key. Initially it may take a little more conscious effort, but the benefits are huge.

anger and victimizers

Unfortunately those who have hidden Anger Wounds seldom seek help unless compelled by a mate, spouse, or the direct intervention of others. Unlike many other hidden wounds, anger finds its primary expression through the victimizer polarity. Victimizers can be defined as those who feel that "might makes right." Usually aggressive, the victimizer polarity is more overtly displayed by men than women.

Because anger has a basis in fear and hurt, to begin the healing process you have to first face and recognize the underlying fear and insecurity. This is easier said than done, especially since the payoff for reactively angry people is that others tend to accommodate them.

I've coached many corporate executives who have been sent to me for management and leadership training. For some, in spite of their effectiveness at accomplishing certain financial goals for their company, their identified problem is usually an insensitive or abusive management style that leaves too many bodies in the wake. Petty tyrants—those who lead by intimidation and do not understand the value of compassionate leadership and empowerment—fall into this category. They are proud of their accomplishments but don't realize that they are driven by hidden Anger Wounds. Others around them become the victims of their wrath and eventually this type of executive is either fired or sent for management training, often termed "charm school." Without the proper insight, for them, "charm" may be seen as just another tool to manipulate rather than to empower others.

I've found that beneath the anger of those who relate to others through the victimizer expression of power is an ever-present fear of vulnerability and pain. It takes great courage to live through the heart. It's much easier in the short term to let your mind be in charge. The various expressions of anger most often begin with your mind seemingly in firm control. The antidote for anger has to do with the heart.

At times, I'll ask a senior executive, known for having a rule-through-intimidation style, if he holds team-building meetings. If so, I usually discover that he leads these meetings by pointing out the failures or shortcomings of others. In so doing, he makes himself seem beyond reproach. This only increases the atmosphere of fear and intimidation among those who directly report to him or her.

In these cases I often suggest that the executive begin such meetings by first sharing a story of his own management failures or mistakes and how he has learned from these experiences. In this way he will create a bond with others that is based on empathy and understanding. This heart-centered, leadership technique also serves to humanize an executive who carries idealized projections from others that are unrealistic and tend to heighten their intimidation of others.

When persisted in, anger is like a smoldering fire that slowly consumes one's health and vitality. It constricts the heart, limits creativity and humor, and closes down any sense of joy or enthusiasm for life and living.

Karmicly speaking, anger is never justified. Even though in some situations anger is an understandable emotion, there is no penance for its expression. The law of karma does not forgive justified expressions of anger no matter how acceptable they may seem from a human perspective. We pay for using anger as a response. To think otherwise is like believing there are cases when fire doesn't burn.

When required for someone's spiritual growth, even the great spiritual masters express only mock anger to impact a devotee. Marpa the Translator, teacher of the renowned eleventh century Tibetan Buddhist Saint Milarepa, was known to use feigned anger during the early years of testing and training his student. Unknown to Milarepa at the time, he was one of Marpa's most loved and cherished devotees. There is no karmic incursion when the expression of such "divine wrath" is directed by spirit, because this is not an ego-directed impulse. Yet it is a mistake to assume that an ego-directed use of mock anger can get results without consequences. Such a deliberate use of mocked anger would just be another form of control and manipulation.

how to manage anger wounds

Certainly anger in its common expression is a human reaction to pain, fear, or loss of control. The question then arises: How do you manage your psyche when anger wells up? Certainly suppression isn't a healthy or effective option. Such strategies, over time, are one of the known causes of stress and depression.

The first mistake many people make is to feel justified in holding on to anger or resentment. Holding on to anger is like embracing a slow-burning ember. Like children, if we let anger emerge and pass quickly, there is minimal backwash, leaving little trace or residue. Watching children at play, as they quickly go through a range of emotions, is a good model for consciously handling states of anger.

Unfortunately anger often gets paired with judgment, self-righteousness, blame, or victimization and causes us to feel justified in its use and maintenance. Additionally when there are hidden Anger Wounds in the unconscious from this and past lives, the triggers are often beyond our control. In spite of our best efforts we find ourselves lashing out with little provocation. That is why it's so important to discover hidden Anger Wounds and release them through Soul Journeys therapy.

hidden anger in relationships

Conrad is an example of someone whose life and relationships were affected by an invisible Anger Wound. He was a tall, solidly built man in his mid-forties with his own successful company; a company that afforded Conrad a lifestyle, which included a private jet that would have been the envy of many.

Conrad came to my office with his longtime girlfriend, Cecily. During my sessions with Conrad, Cecily would usually sit outside in the waiting room of the office. Conrad and Cecily had experienced many challenges in their relationship. Conrad was very high-strung with a strong voice and direct manner. Not only did he have trust issues in the relationship with his girlfriend, he also could be verbally abusive, insensitive, harsh, and moody. He had an explosive temper and seemed constantly on edge, almost hyper-vigilant.

Fortunately, Conrad understood that he needed help to resolve some of these issues and had been through quite a bit of therapy before we met. For years, Conrad had seen a psychoanalyst and had also done Primal Scream therapy with its founder, Arthur Janov. However, Conrad still felt something had been missed in his healing process. There was no doubt, based on his continued angry outbursts, that in spite of all the previous therapy, certain core issues had not been resolved.

During my intake interview with Conrad, I had the feeling that something significant in his childhood was still unresolved. My intuition went against all logic, since Conrad's previous psychoanalysis had combed his childhood backwards and forwards. But still I had the nagging feeling something remained uncovered.

Following that hunch, I started the initial Soul Journeys work by looking for present-life childhood trauma. This approach can identify and resolve trauma even in our present-life that often escapes notice using more traditional forms of therapy. It didn't take but a few minutes to land right in the thick of it. Conrad found himself as a five-year-old boy in the midst of an incest episode with his father. He was being made to perform oral sex. The grief and confusion he experienced was apparent by the intensity of his expressions, verbalizations, and movements on my office sofa. We went through recalling several repeat incest incidents with his father that had occurred during Conrad's childhood.

Although Conrad had arrived feeling healthy during this first session, while he relived the incest incidents, he went through a complete box of Kleenex tissues, filling each with mucus he coughed up. His body was mirroring and regurgitating a physical manifestation of what he had taken in as a child. At a later visit and Soul Journeys session, we also uncovered an incest incident with his mother that had occurred during times while she bathed him.

Conrad had the unfortunate experience of being the victim of incest with both his parents. Yet, there was more.

After resolving and discharging the emotion of the childhood incest, we continued into past lives.

conrad's sources of anger

Conrad's first past life found him as a 12-year-old blind girl living somewhere in the United States during the pioneer days. One morning, her parents had to leave for the day and told her to be careful and stay inside while they were gone. Hours later, a drifter happened by the house and requested water for his horse. At first, the blind girl refused to open the door to take him to the well behind the barn. When the drifter was persistent, she relented and agreed to take him out back.

After realizing this young girl was blind, the drifter took advantage of her by raping her in the barn and then choking her to death. For Conrad, this memory involved reliving sexual abuse, compounded by the trauma of a painful death.

After Conrad recalled his experience as the blind girl, he also released the emotions around two other past-life incidents. They were both tied to a pattern of sexual abuse and trauma that he had to reexperience and resolve if Conrad ever hoped to heal his Anger Wound.

After these Soul Journeys sessions, we could find no other incidents of sexual abuse trauma active in Conrad's psyche. However, he was still simmering at the thought that both of his parents could be so abusive toward him when he was a young boy. To help defuse this anger of victimization, I decided to take Conrad to the lifetime that resulted in his later patterns of victimization. My suspicion was that he would discover a lifetime where he himself was the victimizer. However, I refrained from suggesting this possibility to him.

from victim to victimizer

As we began our next session, the focus of my direction with Conrad was to identify the lifetime responsible for his long cycle of being sexually victimized. With only this direction as a key to our search, Conrad's psyche took us directly to a lifetime preceding the others.

In this past life, Conrad described himself as being the one who had been sexually abusive to others. With an immediate "Ah-ha" response and a touch of humor, Conrad described himself in that lifetime as sexually abusive to young girls and boys. The touch of humor resulted from the irony of Conrad's sudden realization that he had been so disgustingly perverted in a past life but was so judgmental of sexual abusers in this life. The extent of his own hypocrisy at that point seemed comical to him. He could clearly see that the cycle of sexual abuse and wounding, which he had experienced in later lifetimes, had been the flip side of the pain and trauma he had inflicted on others in a previous lifetime. The balance of karmic scales had been just and exacting.

With that realization, the fire of Conrad's anger toward his parents completely died out. He realized that they had been willing yet unconscious instruments for helping him to repay a karmic debt he had incurred. Conrad and his parents were involved in a Karmic Debit Relationship.

My series of sessions with Conrad transformed him in many ways. First, he found himself being less anxious and reactive in life and with his girlfriend, Cecily. His angry edginess and quick temper mellowed, leaving him more willing to consider the needs and feelings of others.

A lazy esophagus, which had been forcing him to sleep with his head and back elevated, was remarkably relieved after our initial session. He could now sleep fully reclined. Finally, Conrad seemed able to relax from his driven, type-A pace of living. No longer was he so quick to project blame and judgment onto others for perceived or imagined faults.

These and other changes in Conrad were very apparent to Cecily, whom he loved dearly. Without her intervention he may never have sought additional therapy for his toxic state of being.

Now that Conrad had recalled *and* relived sexual molestation by both of his parents, was he ready to take them to court? A popular concern today regarding childhood incest is the validity of such accounts, remembered years later in a therapist's office. Charges that the victims have flawed memories at times have resulted in legal battles between suspected abuse victims and their abusers. I suspect this acrimony results when accurately recalled incidents of sexual abuse have been brought to consciousness and not fully discharged. Residual and hidden Anger Wounds leave the victim invariably remaining angry and bitter about the pain and trauma that resulted from such incidents.

I make no effort to convince or deny the validity of my adult clients' childhood memories. My concern is only that we get therapeutic results. When the results are achieved, they can view such incidents as literal or metaphorical.

With the numerous cases I've seen while resolving the trauma of childhood incest and molestation, none have shown an interest in taking legal action against the so-called abusers.

If a client still had the motivation to take legal action against a childhood molester, I would not consider my work finished, because this would be a symptom that the person still has a hidden Anger Wound. I believe that therapists, themselves, play a big factor in whether such motivations for "justice" get resolved in the therapy office or courtroom.

no innocent victims

It's a common understanding in the field of psychology that those, who have been sexually abused as children, often grow up to be abusers themselves. This is often the case unless the abuse victims get help with resolving the pain and trauma of their own sexual abuse.

However, the question remains: Why do such individuals get abused themselves at such an early age of innocence? Why would they be born to endure such circumstances? As I have found over and over again, and as Conrad's story bears out, there are no innocent victims. With nearly all the people I see, I'm quick to point out that by the time they have come to seek the deeper karmic understanding and resolution of the challenges in this life, they have nearly been and done it all in past lives.

All of us have been victimizer and victim with many varied faces. Finally we have come to a point in the karmic cycle where we are looking for avenues to spiritual wholeness. Life may appear unjust to the casual observer, but below the surface, there are always karmic reasons for everything.

Hidden Anger Wound Checklist

You can use the checklist below to determine if you have a hidden Anger Wound that is preventing you from experiencing life in a calm and fulfilling manner.

- Do you find that you often have strong opinions and judgments about everybody and everything?

- Are you frequently suspicious and untrusting of the motives of those around you?

- When challenged or questioned, do you quickly lash out at others?

- Do you take pleasure or get satisfaction putting another in his place or getting retribution for a perceived slight?

- Do you frequently use sarcasm, blame, or shame toward another in the presence of peers or in private?

- Do you find that you rarely if ever apologize for anything?

- Do you easily see the faults in others but rarely see or admit them in yourself?

- Do you get easily upset when your expectations or demands are not met?

- Are you prone to road rage when driving?

- Do you often dream of being in wars and battles where you aggressively attack and destroy adversaries?

- While watching movies or scenes of conflict or assault, do you usually identify with the aggressor?

- Do you find it difficult to forgive a past slight or perceived injustice?

If you answered "yes" to any four out of the twelve questions, you have active Anger Wounds within your psyche.

Even though the roots of these wounds may reside deep in your past, the patterns of anger are reinforced in the present by your reactions to daily occurrences.

To break up the vicious karmic cycle and begin to surface core Anger Wounds, you must begin to regulate your thoughts and actions. Having the intent of *being harmless* with all that you do and say will limit the continued self-destructiveness of the Anger Wound. What *being harmless* implies is that, karmicly speaking, anger is sadistic and masochistic in nature. It can wound those it's directed toward and it is also self-wounding. To *be harmless* is to be unwilling to say or do things that are known to cause pain or injury to another.

the anger meditation

- Find a comfortable, quiet place to sit undisturbed for approximately 20 minutes.

- Close your eyes.

- Take several deep breaths.

- One-by-one, imagine all the people toward whom you have unresolved anger.

Think about each person and try to identify the fears behind your anger. For example, when you see this person, what are you afraid of that makes you angry? Are you afraid of betrayal, hurt, abandonment, or even something involving money? Your fear is usually due to some emotional pain, physical survival, or loss.

Decide if you need to support or maintain that fear, or can you let it go? Is the fear life-threatening? Are you not really going to survive if this person continues the pattern, or is your fear based on not getting what you want or need?

Let your imagination wander to other real or fanciful situations that surface in relation to this fear. Your aim is to get in touch with the fear behind the anger. This is the first step toward self-understanding.

After identifying various undesirable situations, if you find you can't let go of the fear, this indicates that there are deeper past-life roots of your hidden wounds. In this case, recognizing these deeper roots will give you an edge on maintaining your composure, whenever your anger pattern is triggered.

In the next chapter, we're going to explore the Worry and Confusion Wounds. When these wounds are invisible, they can cause paralysis and inertia in spite of your best efforts to motivate yourself. Over time, Worry and Confusion Wounds cause energy-drains and fatigue. Resolving them allows you to have a more purposeful and energetic life.

chapter 8

The Worry and Confusion Wounds

Some of the most successful people have a fear deep down inside that they are not good enough. Other's fear that they will be revealed to be frauds, lacking true competence in their chosen work or profession. They seek the approval of others and the world for most of what they do. These characteristics appear in a person who has either or both Worry and Confusion Wounds.

One expression of Worry and Confusion Wounds finds the individual compulsively doing, and the other plunges a person into a state of paralysis, unable to get much of anything done. In either case people with invisible Worry and Confusion Wounds have difficulty just being. They do not feel that they deserve love and acceptance in the world by the fact of their mere existence. They are constantly trying to justify their value to themselves and to others. They are under the delusion that if they accomplish enough, they will feel the peace and fulfillment they desire. But nothing they do is ever enough.

trouble accepting love

The core problem here is one of love. Even though Worry and Confusion Wound people may be loved, they have difficulty accepting it or they mistrust love. Even the love they give is based on a need to belong and feel accepted. Theirs is love with a hidden agenda and therefore, conditional. Worry and Confusion Wound people give the love they long to receive but can't accept. More frustration results as they imprison themselves inside their own feelings of deprivation and distrust.

The feelings and behaviors of people who don't believe they are worthy of being loved cause an underlying insecurity. Worry constantly activates all manner of fears and wounds from past experiences in their current lifetime as well as unconscious pain from past lives. Worry and Confusion Wounds result in people having hidden anxieties that make them run from one thing to the other in a frenzied quest for fulfillment or freeze in place, unable to move in any significant direction.

Worry and Confusion Wounds cause an inability to live fully in the present because of preoccupation with the past or anticipated future. People with these hidden wounds can be driven and often seek medication to manage the anxiety they feel. They are on a quest for the kind of comfort that comes with recognition of the spiritual self, or soul, but they don't know this is what they're seeking. Spiritual comfort and peace can never be found in the *doing* but only in recognition of *being*. To *Be* requires the ability to openly accept love from others, and in time the universal love that results from pure "Beingness."

the source of worry and confusion wounds

I've found that Worry and Confusion Wounds often begin in the womb before birth. Many young mothers become pregnant unexpectedly with no desire to have a child or they are simply not ready for motherhood. An unwanted pregnancy has a strong impact on the child the mother carries. The result of such unwanted pregnancies, even when unintentional, is the mother's rejection of the child while still in her womb. This initial rejection and everything else that goes on for the mother while she is pregnant leave footprints in the child's psyche that can strongly influence patterns of behavior later in life.

I've mentioned the negative impact on self-acceptance and self-worth that such unwanted pregnancies can have, but many other wounds can also get reinforced during the prenatal period. Some of these are sexual attitudes and responses in relationships, addictive patterns, and a vast array of physical symptoms that are sometimes falsely attributed to genetics.

mary's worry and confusion wounds

To give you some idea of how detailed and complete the imprints from your prenatal period are on your psyche, I'll use Mary's story as an example.

Mary is a successful young insurance representative who lives in the San Francisco area. She's happily married and the mother of a four-year-old girl. Mary's success as an insurance representative was partly due to her anxious energy that drove her to network and perform. She was very good at doing, but probably the only thing she slowed down for was a cup of coffee.

Although not introspective in any way, Mary had another agenda for coming to see me. Having been given up for adoption without delay after her birth, Mary had many unanswered questions about her heritage. Her unconscious questions for her birth mother may have been: *Why was she not kept? Was she loved?*

She had wanted to meet her birth mother, and these feelings only became stronger after the birth of her own daughter.

The problem was that Mary had little, if any, information with which to begin her search. She was also concerned about what impact meeting her biological parents might have on her and all the families involved. Fortunately Mary's adoptive parents, whom she loved very much, were understanding and accepting of her desire to find and meet her birth mother.

Through a friend, Mary had heard of my work. However, her request was unique. Sitting in my office she said, "I know this might sound like an odd request, but I am wondering if you could take me back to my birth to find out anything about my birth mother." I told her that it was indeed unusual to reexperience the birth primarily to attain information, but that it couldn't hurt to try.

From the nine-month prenatal continuing on through birth, the soul can access a complete record of the mother's experiences, thoughts, and feelings. These are imprinted on what may be a cellular level within the fetus even before the neural net has developed completely. Furthermore, the soul does not seem to be limited to the perceptions of the mother while the fetus is in the womb. My experience is that some souls are in and out of the womb during the pregnancy and do not stabilize within the body until the birth occurs. Because of this constant movement, the soul can perceive events surrounding the mother during the course of pregnancy that may have even escaped her awareness. I've even had clients who observed the content of their mothers' dreams during pregnancy, as if they were watching a movie.

mary views her mother's pregnancy

Knowing that the birth experience is often a traumatic one, I decided to ease Mary up to that moment by starting with some incidents that happened to her mother while

Mary's body was forming as a fetus in the womb. We began by going back to around the second month of gestation, when her mother first realized she was pregnant. This is typically the time during an unexpected and unwanted pregnancy, when a mother experiences the greatest reactive fear and may be having thoughts of rejecting her unborn child. Often there are also fears of being rejected by others when a woman has an unwanted pregnancy. Mary's mother was no exception.

In this part of the Soul Journey, Mary saw her mother standing in her bedroom, feeling a little nauseous, fearing that she is pregnant. She is fifteen and panicked. She doesn't know what to do, only that it will not be a happy moment when she breaks the news to her parents. So she puts it off. While Mary is viewing her mother in the bedroom, I have her, as yet unborn, describe furnishings such as the dresser, bed, and chairs in the room. My intent early on in this session was to get Mary accustomed to noticing minute details.

Remember from Chapter 2 how the soul can take a panoramic view of it's surroundings in any past-life experience, unencumbered by the limited perceptions the conscious mind had at the time?

In the next part of her Soul Journey, Mary went to a later point during her mother's pregnancy. It was around the fifth month, which happened to be summer. At this point, Mary's mother and her boyfriend stand in the living room of her parent's home, facing her mother, father, and grandmother. Mary's mother is petrified of telling her parents the news, but she knows that she can't hide the pregnancy any longer.

Through her mother's eyes and consciousness, Mary described the tense scene she witnessed, as soul, even though she was only a fetus when it actually happened. She sees the living room in detail: Her 17-year-old father stands in the hallway as her mother tells her parents she is pregnant. They are not supportive. They insist that the two must get married and make plans to drive them to a neighboring state, where marriage is legal at their young ages.

Finally, I guided Mary to her birth, where she sees herself as an infant just coming out of the womb. She described the shock of cold air and bright lights as she is brought into the world. For the first time she gets a look at her biological mother's face and feels the warmth of her embrace as she is briefly given to her to hold.

Then I asked Mary to focus closely on everything she could see and hear in the delivery room. She reads nametags on the doctors' and nurses' uniforms and describes how they prep her after she is born. Then she hears her mother's name being spoken by the doctor: "Marsha."

I told Mary to repeat the name several times for clarification. I asked her if she could tell me the last name and she eventually said, "Marsha Powers."

the search is on

Armed with the name of her biological mother, Mary began her search. Due to sealed birth records, she had never been told her mother's name, but fortunately she did know the city and state of her own birth. She hired a private detective who quickly located her birth mother in the Pacific Northwest. He gave Mary a phone number so she could contact her mother at home.

When I next saw Mary in my office, we discussed her anticipation and anxiety about making a call to the mother she had never known. Finally she felt ready for whatever the outcome would be and made an initial phone contact.

Mary's birth mother was surprised and delighted, telling her daughter that she had been praying for this day. "It was really a fairy tale," Mary told me. "My birth mother said all the right things." Soon after talking with her mother, Mary booked a flight to meet her in person.

The moment of finally coming face-to-face with her mother was one of indescribable joy, a very deep and somehow spiritual experience that Mary could scarcely find words to express.

When they met, Mary described to Marsha the bedroom she had seen during her Soul Journeys session with me. This had been where Marsha first realized she was pregnant as a frightened and confused young woman. She then described the living room and the conversation in which her mother had delivered the news of her pregnancy to her parents and grandmother.

Marsha, although a little taken aback by such a clear description, confirmed every detail. Both women were astounded by the accuracy of Mary's descriptions of these places she had no way of seeing or hearing of.

With the help of her mother, Mary continued her search. She found her biological father, who also resides on the West Coast. Mary told me she had a wonderful reunion with her biological father. He corroborated the scene in which Marsha told her family that she was pregnant. When she asked her father why he had stood in the hallway of the living room while her mom delivered the news, he explained that he felt like an outsider with her parents because of his Latin heritage.

Today, Mary maintains contact with both of her biological parents. They're happy to know that their daughter has gone on to establish a family of her own.

In the years since, she and her family have moved to the East Coast. She remains happily married and is involved with a career in politics.

In Mary's case, her primary therapeutic goal was to learn about and meet her birth mother. However, as is often the case, other goals are apparent to the therapist, and they are of equal importance. Going through Mary's prenatal experience we were not only able to get the name of her birth mother, but we were also able to release imprinted emotions and thoughts of fear and rejection her mother had felt while pregnant. In a situation like this, the shift from a lack of comfort with a person's self-worth and acceptance to a greater sense of it is so natural that it often goes unnoticed when the person is not acutely aware of the problem. Mary's success in the world overshadowed her awareness of a need to be accepted and wanted. Fortunately she also had a very loving husband. As a result, the joy and acceptance she experienced meeting her birth parents was reward enough for our efforts, but I noticed deeper benefits in her. She was now much more content just being Mary.

resolving worry and confusion from prenatal messages

Unique as Mary's experience may seem, such recall of events, whether from the prenatal, birth, or past lives, is common when doing Soul Journeys sessions. In Mary's example, the focus was primarily on extracting information for the purpose of reuniting a mother and daughter. The need to resolve messages of fear or rejection from the prenatal period was a valuable but secondary outcome. Uncovering hidden Worry and Confusion Wounds is usually primary and in many cases, a great necessity in the healing process.

An example of when the need to resolve prenatal messages becomes primary is demonstrated in Lois's case. She came to me to help her improve her ability to communicate with her husband, Nate.

A tall, friendly woman with brown, shoulder length hair and a warm presence, Lois had a successful career as an interior decorator. Nate also had his own successful business with an office in their home.

Even though her marriage was stable, Lois felt stagnant in the relationship. She often found herself hesitating to fully express to her husband how she was feeling. Lois had difficulty clearly stating her thoughts and feelings to others, especially to men. Her tendency was to anticipate the needs and expectations of those around her and spin her words to accommodate them.

Additionally Lois could not watch any type of violence on TV or movies and on occasion, would get sinus headaches that turned into migraines. During my initial intake session with Lois, it was clear that she had low self-esteem and self-worth. She compensated by putting the needs of everyone else before her own. Lois's fundamental issue was a lack of self-love with an underlying fear of rejection. These are classic symptoms of hidden Worry and Confusion Wounds.

Because of Lois's emerging profile during the intake interview, I asked specific questions regarding her birth. She knew very little about her birth other than that she was the youngest of four children, and her birth had been the result of an unplanned pregnancy.

It was apparent that with Lois we should begin our work in the prenatal period to locate and resolve any negative messages she unconsciously carried from her mother's experience of being pregnant. Self-esteem and self-worth issues are usually a telltale sign of some type of prenatal or birth trauma.

lois remembers rejection

We began the Soul Journeys session with Lois lying on the sofa in my office, reliving her mother's first realization that she was pregnant.

Lois could see her mother standing at the window in her bedroom saying, "Damn it! I can't be pregnant. This is not what I wanted. How are we going to do this financially? I just can't be pregnant. What am I going to do?" With that, Lois's mother put her hands over her face and started to cry. Slowly she walked away from the window.

Lois then shifted to when her mother first told her father she is pregnant. The couple is sitting at the kitchen table. Lois's mother simply says, "I'm pregnant again. Now, how are we going to deal with this? We can't take care of the ones we have.

On another occasion during the pregnancy, Lois's mother is in the house doing chores and thinking: I don't want to have this baby and I don't want to take care of another baby. I've had to do that all my life. I don't want you and I never wanted you. At that point, someone comes to the door and her mother has company.

Moving forward to one evening in the seventh month of the pregnancy, Lois observes her mother lying on her right side in the bed. Lois recounted her mother's thoughts: He doesn't want me because I'm ugly and fat. I'm tired of dealing with all of this.

Later in the eighth month, Lois watched her mother ironing and yelling at her dad. It's late in the evening, and he has just come home. She says, "Where have you been? You've been drinking. I can tell you've been drinking. You said you were coming right home. Who were you with?"

Lois's mother then walks away from him and thinks about her husband and unborn child: He doesn't love me. He's never loved me. Nobody loves me. I hate you.

damaging and unfiltered messages to the unconscious

Messages, such as the ones Lois received from her mother combined with the emotional charges gripping the mother, go unfiltered straight into the unconscious of the child she is carrying in the womb. The unconscious of the child does not put them into context as the mother's thoughts and feelings but records them as literal messages. Later, as the child matures into adulthood, these messages are automatically triggered when the person is feeling fear or stress. The messages replay themselves below the surface of consciousness as Worry and Confusion Wounds. They are like quiet whisperings in the psyche that zap self-confidence and self-acceptance.

We are constantly trying to find ways to compensate for the effects of such corrosive messages with rationalizations, positive affirmations, drugs, and medications. My experience is that these strategies only serve as temporary Band-Aids and are no longer needed once the negative messages are brought to consciousness and discharged.

In Lois's case, the final phase of her Soul Journeys session involved shifting to Lois's mother in the hospital where she was taken to the delivery room. Her water had broken minutes before while she sat on a stool in a café with her husband. Suddenly she said to him, "Oh my god, I can't believe I just did that. I'm so embarrassed. We've got to go to the hospital."

In the hospital, Lois's mother gave birth to her during a difficult delivery. The doctor had to use forceps to get her out of the womb. Lois described feeling forceps clamp down over her right eye and behind her head on the left side, as they dragged her out of the womb.

When I heard Lois describing her birthing experience, I was reminded that besides resolving her fear of rejection and self-esteem, Lois had also been having a problem with migraines. Forceps deliveries are often a causal or contributing factor with such headaches.

After she was out of the womb, Lois described a nurse holding her and saying, "She's so beautiful and little. I wish she were mine." This was the first time she received positive messages of love and acceptance. She was then handed over to her mother and felt disconnected, compared to the warm and nurturing presence of the nurse.

more sources of invisible worry and confusion for lois

The other Soul Journeys sessions I had with Lois took us more directly into previous lifetimes where she had a couple of startling revelations.

She discovered that in her previous life, she had been the wife of her grandfather. She also learned that in that same past life, her mother in this lifetime had been her three-year-old daughter back then.

This had been a very difficult and abusive lifetime with a husband who was an alcoholic. Lois's Soul Journey revealed that one afternoon, while the wife had been pregnant with her fourth child, her drunken husband had beaten her and forced himself upon her sexually. Hours later, too weak to call for help, she had a miscarriage that resulted in her bleeding to death alone. Her six-year-old son found her body curled up in the corner of the family's outhouse and he ran to the neighbors for help.

The woman Lois had been was 35 years old when she died in that previous lifetime. Her daughter was the youngest of her three children. Lois understood that in that life, the trauma of losing her mother was greatest for this daughter. The little girl's terrible grief was one of the reasons the soul that became Lois chose to reincarnate as the child of her past-life daughter.

Unfortunately, Lois also brought her own wounds into her current life from that previous life with an abusive husband. Her willingness in that life to accept physical and emotional abuse contributed to her fear and difficulty in expressing her needs, wants, and expectations with her current husband.

Curiously, during my initial intake interview with Lois, she mentioned that she had quite often felt like a mother to her mother. Lois felt that her mother did not really understand how to be a mother. This was understandable since in the past lifetime, Lois (as her mother's mother) had been snatched away when the child was only three years old.

Lois also told me that, as a little girl in her current life, she had felt uncomfortable with her grandfather. On the few occasions when she saw him before he died, she would not stay in the same room with him. There was no evidence that Lois had ever been abused or molested by her grandfather or anyone else, so this kind of experience wasn't what caused her extreme need to avoid him. All signs pointed to Lois having an unconscious memory of the previous lifetime when her grandfather had been her abusive husband.

In total, I spent approximately six-and-one-half hours with Lois doing Soul Journeys sessions. Months after completing her therapy, Lois reported a significant increase in her self-confidence with little or no fear of rejection. She found herself naturally able to communicate more openly and freely with her husband and others outside of the family. Her newfound confidence allowed Lois to make some important and empowering changes in the way she ran her business and the people associated with it. Unconscious Worry and Confusion Wounds hidden within her psyche were no longer ruling her. Casually, almost as an aside, Lois mentioned that she was no longer plagued with headaches and had not had one in the nine months since our last session.

Prenatal and Birth Wound Checklist

- Do you have a lack of self-confidence, self-esteem, fear of rejection, or need to accommodate or prove your worth to others.

- Did your parents experience physical or emotional conflict during the time you were in the womb?

- Were you or do you suspect your conception was unplanned or unwanted?

- Did your mother experience any type of trauma or major loss during her pregnancy with you?

- Was your mother physically or emotionally abused or injured at any time during her pregnancy with you?

- Were forceps used on you during your mother's delivery?

- Do you frequently have headaches or migraines that start at the same place on your head?

- Were there serious complications during your mother's pregnancy or delivery?

- Was there any abortion attempt by your mother during the pregnancy that you are aware of?

If you answered "yes" to the first and any other three of these nine questions, there is a high probability that you carry unresolved unconscious prenatal or birth wounds.

If you answered yes to five of the nine questions, excluding the first, you likely have unresolved prenatal and birth experiences that are manifesting as hidden Worry and Confusion Wounds. You are compensating for them in some way by your behavior or life choices.

These wounds often have roots in the prenatal and birth period. Accepting one's Beingness often has its start in the present-life through the parents' acceptance of your *Being* during the first realization of pregnancy and the months thereafter. This is the first and maybe only period where, as a fetus in the womb, you are unable to *do* anything. You can only be. To receive love from your parents for just being present is one of the greatest gifts. Later, as you mature, all *doing* grows out of this loving foundation of being accepted.

It's been said by some that, "Soul exists because God loves it." Awareness of this is the final and ultimate experience of Beingness from the source of all existence. If you can mirror that love in your exchanges with others, you are expressing the divine spark within.

chapter 9

The Shame and Guilt Wounds

Now LET'S TAKE A LOOK INTO THE WOUNDS OF SHAME AND GUILT. THESE wounds often hide under the surface of your awareness. People compensate dysfunctionally for Shame and Guilt Wounds by choosing to make others feel shameful and guilty. They typify the old adage: "People who live in glass houses should not throw stones." Hidden Shame and Guilt Wounds often motivate "finger-pointers," who can't see their own Shadows or Dark Sides.

The tests in life come and the tests in life go. They will continue to come and go until we make the grade. What it takes to make the grade is unique for each individual. But the tests of life all seem to revolve around having an understanding response tempered with compassion when relationships or situations change or cause pain.

Once you fully accept this constant spiritual testing process and the principles of karma and reincarnation, there is no need to burden yourself with the extra baggage of shame and guilt. These two emotions are merely the unconscious recognition of the karmic principle of retribution. It's a realization from the soul that we are held accountable for the constructive or destructive things we do. Making this realization fully conscious allows you to take greater responsibility for your actions.

When you fully take responsibility for your actions, shame and guilt serve no useful purpose. On the occasions when you lose touch with your guiding principles by forgetting to do no harm, you just accept that the scales will be balanced somehow and at some time without falling into guilt or shame. Why worry about an automatic process? The self-flagellation of shame and guilt only increases the energetic burden of karma. It's like overpaying a monetary debt because you feel bad about getting into debt. The universe adds interest enough without compounding it unnecessarily.

A good illustration of how present day results can manifest when responsibility is not taken and resolved for actions in the past is shown in Margaret's Soul Journey below. Because she continued to carry the unconscious shame and guilt of being both victim and victimizer from a past life, Margaret suffered from chronic physical ailments in this lifetime.

Margaret was a middle-aged housewife married to an engineer. I learned during my intake interview with her that she had suffered from migraine headaches since she was a teenager. Her life had become absorbed coping with her headaches and maintaining a household. She had been unable to maintain jobs because of her disability. Medication had become a part of her daily ritual to control the pain for years. On occasion she had to be taken to emergency care for morphine injections to relieve the pain.

Margaret also required medication to sleep at night due to the severity of her pain. She had been to migraine specialists, received acupuncture, and numerous other therapies with no relief. Resigned to taking drugs for the foreseeable future she was still open to the possibility that some form of treatment might rid her of her burden of headaches. Margaret's life theme had become pain management.

My first Soul Journey session with Margaret took us to her birth where the doctor had used forceps during the delivery. Unfortunately, this procedure had begun the trauma to her head in this lifetime and had to be released. After two other past-life episodes involving head trauma she experiences a lifetime where she was a brutal French officer leading a proud regiment of soldiers on horseback.

The regiment had attacked a peasant village and was ordered to burn homes and kill many inhabitants including old men, women, and children. His soldiers felt such an assault was not required to take the village but reluctantly agreed. During the attack, he saw a young woman running away with her infant son and dismounted his horse in pursuit on foot. Finally he ran her down and with his sword brutally beheaded her. He also murdered her infant son.

At that point he heard horse hoofs galloping toward him. As he looked, he saw his second in command with sword raised galloping toward him. In a flash he realized his blood lust had turned him into a monster killing-machine. He felt shame and remorse for the brutality that had overtaken him in his need to prove himself in his new command. His first officer was suddenly upon him and brought his sword down on his head for a fatal wound in one quick motion as he rode by on his horse. As a result, he fell over dead and immediately left the body.

His men under the direction of his first in command had been reluctant to carry out his bloody siege on such a defenseless village. Observing his brutal actions in battle, they had decided he was not worthy of their allegiance. Out of body and up above the battlefield he surveyed the carnage and saw that most of his men had observed the brutality he inflicted on the young mother and her son. They rejoiced and ceased the hostility when the first officer killed him. The village had long since been overrun and secured.

Floating above the body, he felt guilt and shame at what he had become. He noticed a light above in the sky that beckoned him but felt unworthy to go to it. He remained earthbound feeling shame and pity for his sins. Margaret describes entering into a gray area for what seems like days or weeks as this disembodied French officer. Finally, a light approached directly toward the officer. As it came closer, he noticed it was the young woman he had slain just before his death. This is how Margaret as a French officer in that life described the experience.

"She comes toward me and I am in shock. I am so ashamed that I can't even look her in the face, but she's so beautiful, radiant, and giving. She takes me by my hands and she is walking backward, leading me into the light. I can't see anything but just feel her love and forgiveness.

"We go into the light and I start feeling better but I still feel shame. As she leads me into the light more people start to surround us. It's all the villagers that I have killed. They are all there to forgive me and I can't believe it. They are all like angels, but I recognize them from the battle when we killed them in the village. She still has me by the hands and she is still looking at me. I start to realize that they have all truly forgiven me and that it is okay. We go more and more into the light and I become light myself and I start to forgive myself. Pretty soon I look just like them. At first, I was still solid looking and in my suit. Now I have more loose clothing on. They are still all surrounding me because they realize that I still need support. She then takes me to see other people I've killed at other times. They are forgiving me too. They just appear and I feel like I am getting lighter. The surrounding is all just light and she is still with me. She shows me other lives when I've been a better person. It's like a movie. She is trying to show me that I haven't always been an evil person. She shows me that I was once a nun and really sweet. I see how in others lives I've served other people.

"I'm told if I ask for forgiveness that I will be forgiven. I'm surprised how simple it is. She says it's not complicated. She introduces me to people whom in other lives I've really helped. They come up to me and they hug me and remind me of the help that I have given them. They are like angels too."

After this session, Margaret experienced significant relief from her migraines. During our next and last session Margaret found herself again as a male. This time she was an English hunchback servant to a householder in London. Unfortunately, the householder was a cruel man who had a drinking problem. On occasion he would get drunk and would blame any problem or misfortune on his hunchback servant. Margaret said that as a hunchback, he was paid less than someone without such a deformity.

One late evening the householder was drunk and angry. He decided to take his wrath out on his hunchback servant and began to beat him with a club outside on the street. Trying to protect himself the hunchback tried to cover up while curled up on the street. With bony protrusions along his spine and the back of his head, his brutal boss' hammering of his body could not be deflected. The bones in his head fractured causing him to die from hemorrhaging.

After this, our fifth and last, session Margaret's headaches ended abruptly. She told me during follow up calls that she had stopped taking all medications and that her migraines had not returned. Nine months later she was still headache free.

Shame and Guilt Wounds Checklist

- Are you hesitant or fearful about asserting yourself for fear that you may hurt or abuse another?

- Are you outraged when you hear about the hurt or injustice to certain individuals or groups?

- Do you feel it's your responsibility and are passionately driven to correct certain injustices occurring in your community or in the world?

- Are you very judgmental of others and prone to self-righteous indignation?

- Do you obsess or lose sleep at the thought that you may have hurt someone or made life difficult for another person?

- Do you tend to root for the underdog?

If you answered "yes" to any three of these six questions, consider Shame and Guilt wounds as part of your emotional baggage and a karmic dynamic in your relationships. You may wish to take a close look at how and when these karmic patterns emerge. You may also recognize that they cause compulsive behavior and reactions that unconsciously drive certain motivations and decisions in your life. Such motivations and decisions can unconsciously drive you to do good in the community or world.

karmic awareness

We often curse or have cursed ourselves with shame and guilt in the past and while living past lives. The basis for invisible Shame and Guilt Wounds usually stems from past failures and abuses of your personal ethics. When you feel shame and guilt because you didn't adhere to a higher ethical standard, this realization suggests a turning point in the education of soul. For it heralds the awareness of a higher ethical or moral standard. This internal standard is a mirror of karmic awareness, which is a more conscious awareness of a truth that the soul knows. Karmic awareness eventually leads to karmic responsibility and greater spiritual insight.

When karmic awareness comes online within your consciousness, then life may start to become more challenging. Awareness and acceptance of the karmic principles in your life and relationships tend to accelerate karmic activity. Such acceleration has its inherent advantages and challenges. The advantage is that you can change or manifest things in your life much more quickly. The challenge is that our missteps also show up much more rapidly. Unlike those stores where no payment or interest is due on purchases for 12 or 24 months, the universe may call in your notes of payment within a shorter period. The principle being that with greater awareness comes greater responsibility.

Your reading this book suggests that you have recognized karmic principles in this or some past life and are now starting to wake up to the rules of the game. It's a game that you will sooner or later win and transcend, no matter how far in debt you appear to be today.

self-responsibility

Shame and guilt may still be part of your burden, but it's now time to examine their usefulness. How do shame and guilt serve you today? Are they like punitive parents riding your back, criticizing every moral or ethical failure? Do you still need such parents to keep your thoughts and behavior in check? How would life be different if you accepted karmic law as fact and just let go of shame and guilt?

The pace of life today has become too fast for most of us to add the stress of extra emotional baggage, but we still do it out of ignorance. When and how do you plan to change that?

Up until now, we've mainly discussed past lives where a person's trauma has been the result of having been victimized by others. In Chapter 7, Conrad's story was one exception to this pattern. It's time now for us to dig a little deeper into how karma influences relationships, especially in regard to hidden Shame and Guilt Wounds.

If you've been following the principles of karma and how they work, you realize that being a victim follows a time when you caused victimization in someone else. More specifically, we have initiated the causes responsible for our misfortunes somewhere in time. As soul, we are aware of this but at a conscious level, we are most often in denial about the victim/victimizer dynamic. It's difficult or next to impossible for most of us to accept that we have caused the misfortunes that befall us—if not in this lifetime, in another. But now, it's time to wake up to that fact.

We can't lose what we have truly earned and we can't keep what we don't deserve. This is karma in action. And it applies to all our relationships.

This principle is the most difficult aspect of karma that we must come to terms with and is quietly omitted in most of the current books dealing with past lives and past-life therapy. Total self-responsibility is not a popular concept because it makes the projection of blame meaningless.

For the spiritually mature, the concept of total self-responsibility can be extraordinarily liberating, but for many others it's an outrageous affront. If you're in the second category, my heart goes out to you. It can be a painful realization to accept. To try and force such acceptance on another is like trying to compress density. It meets great resistance and can result in an angry response. Why bother trying to convince anyone that they are totally responsible for their actions and their lives? Give them love and acceptance instead. You could even lend a helping hand when appropriate. It's much more useful.

shame, guilt, and victimization

Shame and Guilt Wounds are often tied to the victimization polarity of the karmic equation. They are part of the bandwidth in which a person consciously misuses power or authority.

In the case of Conrad he was not able to fully resolve the trauma and anger of being sexually abused until he saw and forgave his own history of being an abuser. Only then, could the internal paradigm shift fully occur within him. The work Conrad did with me helped him to dissolve the density of his anger and relieved him of shame and guilt.

Uncovering the victimizer polarity is not necessary to resolve all past-life trauma, but with certain clients, and especially those who carry unconscious Shame and Guilt Wounds, it's an absolute necessity.

shame, guilt, and the shadow

Shame and guilt stem from our unconscious Shadow Selves and are repressed in service of the ego. I could give you many examples of this dynamic from my case studies but will include only one here to help you gain a better understanding of how a person's life can be affected by invisible wounds.

Sally is an actress with a doctorate in forensic psychology. She initially came with her husband, Julio, the advertising executive with authority figure issues you met in Chapter 3. A petite, very attractive woman in her early 40s, Sally had a positive, optimistic outlook that could clearly sustain her through challenging times. When they arrived for their appointments at my office, they were dressed casually. To avoid influencing Julio's Soul Journeys experience with Sally's, I started the sessions with Sally alone. The following account is only of Sally's experiences, because they have the most bearing on hidden Shame and Guilt Wounds.

One pressing concern Sally had was that her acting career had suddenly come to a standstill and felt blocked. She said it was uncanny how circumstances conspired to keep her away from promising roles. She recounted a series of incidents where she was referred for specific roles, or casting agents seemed poised to give her parts for which she was perfectly suited. Suddenly these opportunities would all unravel in the most improbable ways, as if she had been jinxed. She couldn't understand it but felt the problem was much more than simple coincidence or bad luck. It was as if the universe was conspiring against her acting success, and she was starting to feel desperate.

After getting more information about Sally's history during the initial interview, we began the first Soul Journeys session into a past life.

a roman lifetime of abuse

As she first entered the past-life scene, Sally found her-self in the obese body of a middle-aged man with, as she described, a fat stomach. The man was balding, of medium height, and had a double chin. He was quite a contrast to the shapely, attractive woman Sally is today.

The man wore a light cotton toga held by a rope belt. He had rings on his fingers and wore sandals. He stood laughing at a battle scene being played out in a theater by a troupe of actors.

The theatrical scene was of Roman soldiers trying to overtake peasants who were rising up to beat them. In Sally's words, "The people are happy, laughing, and cheering because the soldiers are losing.

"A little boy backstage beside me wonders if it's his time to perform, and I rub his head and push him out on stage. I then pick up a little white dog near my feet and pet him. I'm mindlessly eating while I stand there, even though I'm not hungry."

As you might surmise from this excerpt, Sally had slipped directly into a past life she had had during the Roman Empire. In that life she was a Roman male, living alone with a little white dog. His house had a dirt floor and rough-hewn furniture. Outside, there was a dirt street, and the houses were packed next to each other with no space between them. Sally described the houses as being very small with only one room and a fireplace.

The Roman man had no friends or steady female com-panionship. He ran a theater that employed a troupe of male and female actors. Many of the actors had families and children to support.

sources of sally's hidden shame and guilt

I guided Sally completely through this past life from the point where it began with her watching the actors from backstage to the Roman's death in that lifetime.

What we learned in that life is that the Roman man was an actor as a youth but at 46 years old, he employed a troupe of 15 to 18 actors in an outdoor theater. In Sally's words, "I'm coldhearted and mean-spirited. I don't have friends or know how to be a friend. I feel that if I intimidate the actors, they will work for less and less money. I hoard the money, thinking I will get rich. The actors cannot work elsewhere, as there is little or no work for actors. I live simply and alone. One or more of the actresses I sleep with, I get pregnant."

Following is an incident Sally described regarding an actress's pregnancy.

"Someone is knocking at my door, and I open it to find a pregnant woman with a child. She is staring at me. She needs money. I slam the door in her face and tell her I owe her nothing. I tell her that the child she is carrying is not mine, even though I know it is. I say, Get off my step, you vermin. She cries and pounds the door. I laugh and am thinking, what an idiot! What do they expect of me? I go and get warm by the fire, because it's cold outside."

Sally told of another day when the Roman man arrived at the theater.

"The actors are there early. One smallish man comes forward. He's slightly built with dark hair, light eyes, and feminine features. He is weak. The young man says that the actors need a bigger percentage. The Roman man walks over to the actor, slaps him, and says, 'I'll tell you what you earn. I decide.' He then twists this small young actor's arm behind his back, dislocating his right shoulder, as the actor falls to the ground. He says, 'you don't threaten me. And if you do, this will happen to you.' The man cries and screams. The Roman man finally slams his foot down on the actor's shoulder and says, 'you'll never do that again. Don't even try.'"

Sally then said of the theater owner, "I pick up the actor by the shoulders, slap him on the back, and tell him not to be a baby. Afterward, the Roman man sits down to eat while he watches his actors rehearse."

Sally pointed out that this young actor is now her daughter, Courtney, in this lifetime, and Courtney has a chronic problem with her right shoulder. And of course, as her mother in this lifetime, Sally has been responsible for Courtney's care.

"One day, the Roman man announces that he is going to close the theater. The troupe is in shock about this. Fed up with his abuse, one night while the cruel man is out, an actor disguises himself and breaks into the Roman man's home. When the owner returns and opens his door, the man puts a knife to his throat. As they stumble to the bed, the attacker says, 'you are not going to put us out. We have to earn a living. We have children to raise and feed.' During this incident the Roman man becomes so frightened, he urinates on himself and tells his assailant, 'Okay, anything you want.' Afterward, he realizes that his neck has been slightly cut and even his dog had been poisoned. He starts crying and thinks, 'I'm scared. I could have died. I'll get that s.o.b. I know who it is.'"

"Later, after a performance the actors are expecting their money, and the theater owner tells them, 'Nope, I'm not giving you anything. That's what you get for your insolence. I'm shutting down the theater.' He then starts to kick and break down the sets saying, 'Nobody tells me what to do.'"

more shame and guilt wounds for sally

The next incident Sally described is when the theater owner got drunk one night in a bar that is crowded with other men and prostitutes.

He tells someone in the bar that he's going to be rich because he stole money from the actors. Sally then said, "He buys a prostitute but can't perform. She laughs at him. He slaps her around and leaves."

She then described a scene, which happened the same night.

The theater owner is drunk. He sits in the street, throwing up on himself. Sally said, "I spit up blood, cough, and my chest feels tight. I have TB, and my teeth are bad. I can't get warm, but I make myself feel better by thinking that I'll be rich before I die."

On his way home the man sees that his house is on fire. He thinks, "those bastards. They burned my house down." Unfortunately, the whole row of houses burns down, putting families and kids out on the street. The actors' money burns in the fire, and the actors are all angry with him. He cries while the people in the village blame him for the fire. Blaming the Roman theater owner for the fire is the villagers' way of trying to extract revenge on him, because they all know about his theft and abuse of the actors.

As the houses burn, the villagers approach the theater owner and start to kick, beat, and stone him. Eventually he finds himself facedown in the mud, being stoned to death and choking. As he dies he thinks, "I don't have any friends. I'm dying alone. I curse you all." While dying, he also realizes that everyone in the neighborhood knows how he has treated his actors. They know he kept their money and they hate him for it. In the end he thinks, "I don't want to be homeless. I don't want to be friendless. I don't want to die sick and I don't want to die being hated." Yet he dies facedown in the mud.

As you can see, Sally's life as the Roman man ended miserably. This man had abused what little power he had by being cold, insensitive, and dishonest. My task with Sally at that point was to find a way for her to forgive herself. Fully resolving the trauma of a life, such as the one she recalled, has a natural clearing effect. Yet it was obvious that Sally carried unconsciousness guilt and shame from that past life into her present one. This was probably responsible for her sudden lack of success as an actor in Los Angeles.

Why was Sally's acting success suddenly arrested?

Whatever the karmic repercussions of that past life, as an aspiring actor in this life, Sally carried the added burden of shame and guilt in her unconscious. That alone could sabotage her efforts at success. Since the unconscious makes links through direct association, the very thought of acting activates the unconscious past-life energy of guilt, shame, failure, and disgrace. In my experience, even the energy you carry regarding an activity, project, or relationship affects others to your advantage or disadvantage. They unconsciously become tools for karmic balance simply because your energy can raise either doubt or generate immediate interest and acceptance. You must remember that karma is energy and the whole universe is based on energetic interactions without limit to space or time.

inciting events that cause wounds to resurface

Often certain emotionally charged past lives will activate suddenly with a certain incident or event that happens in your present life. It's like the karmic energy of that past life is time-released and gets triggered at a certain predestined time.

In Sally's case, to fully resolve this past-life trauma, I realized it would help to determine why the man, whom she was in that lifetime, had grown so mean and bitter.

What we discovered was that in that life the theater owner had been the son of teenage, peasant parents in Rome who didn't have enough money for survival.

Sally described what happened one day, when the Roman man had been a five-year-old boy in that lifetime.

"We are in an open air marketplace, and I'm with my parents. I know how to steal. My parents steal food and put it in my clothes. We think nobody will suspect us, but the vendors notice and alert the police who are walking around. They take the food out of my clothes and arrest my parents. They insist that they didn't do anything, but the police search me and find all kinds of things we've stolen.

"The police then throw up two quick crosses. They tie my parents' hands to the crosses and slit their throats. They say, 'This is what will happen to you if you continue stealing.'

I hit the police, and they slap and push me away. I'm kneeling at the base of the crosses and crying. I don't want to be alone. I want to have a friend. At that moment, I just stop caring."

Sally recognized her parents then as the same parents she has in this lifetime. She also commented that her father today even has a similar type of Roman nose.

Given the experiences as a young boy in Rome, it's understandable why this child grew up to be such a bitter and abusive employer.

With Sally's invisible Shame and Guilt Wounds, as with all wounds of this nature, self-forgiveness is the main issue. The curse the Roman man directed toward the actors in that past life was essentially a curse carried forward and crippling Sally's psyche in this lifetime. To undo such a curse requires that the person forgive others and themselves.

Finally, after seeing her whole past-life picture, Sally understood the source of her shame and guilt. She forgave herself for being such a lout as the Roman theater owner. With this forgiveness, she experienced a sensation of relief and lightness, as if the whole karmic pattern was dissolving.

dissolving remnants and residues

After the emotions around traumatic past lives are resolved, I most often take my clients into the Past-Life Museum that I will describe in the next chapter. There, we are able to dissolve remnants and residues from past lives in what some might consider an imagined flow of light and sound. This process is much like radiation or chemotherapy that kills cancerous cells in the body after a tumor is removed but without the toxic side effects.

On occasion, I've had those who have allowed themselves to be continually taken advantage of in relationships or even abused in work situations because they are too passive, conciliatory, or simply not appropriately aggressive. They restrain themselves because they fear that they might abuse power and cause harm, often sabotaging their own success.

In most cases these are the most considerate people you can imagine. To the outside observer their fear of abusing others would seem highly irrational. Upon closer examination we find that they are overcompensating for a past-life abuse of power, which they still carry as a memory in their unconscious. In these situations no amount of reasoning will convince them to be more neutral about their use of power. They can't seem to accept that their strong sense of compassion and fairness will keep them from being seduced into abusing power. Again, in Soul Journeys therapy we must go to the source of these fears to free them of unconscious shame and guilt. There we often find a past-life abuse of power as an expression of their shadow.

In my follow up with Sally I learned that, after our Soul Journeys therapy sessions, she experienced a marked change in her acting career. Finally things had opened up, and she was getting work again. Because her karmic energy had changed around her role as an actor all those involved with giving her acting roles also experienced an energetic shift.

She realized that unconscious Shame and Guilt Wounds were holding her back. In her marriage these wounds had resulted in a hypersensitivity and anger if there was any suggestion of a lack of consideration by her husband. Now she was much more relaxed and less reactive about Julio's behavior. In turn, because of Sally's energetic shift, Julio was more considerate. Fortunately for her, Julio had it within him to be more considerate.

When you can understand and agree with the Roman poet Terence who said, "Nothing human is foreign to me," you have reached a stage where soul is asserting itself with compassion and understanding in spite of the temptation to judge or project blame. Reactive strategies of anger and blame result in back-steps instead of allowing you to move forward into wholeness.

chapter 10

The Soul Journeys Process

THERE ARE SEVERAL METHODS I USE TO ACCESS PAST LIVES AND BEGIN A Soul Journey. In this chapter, you will have an opportunity to review and apply a simplified version of the Soul Journeys method I use. It's proven effective time and again for catching a glimpse of past lives. I call it the Past-Life Museum. It's called this because nearly all of my clients experience this hall of past lives as having a museum like appearance. I might also add that this museum was not an imagined construct I myself created to review past lives.

Years ago one of my early clients stumbled into this inner structure during one of our past-life sessions. Therapeutically it was like finding a gold mine. From that day forward, whenever I would suggest this museum to clients they could go there without difficulty, as if it were an actual place. What I've found is that the museum method for past-life recall provides a familiar base for the soul to preview many lives more objectively without direct engagement. From there, entry into a specific past or possible future life is simply a matter of choice. For many years, this method has demonstrated its reliability for thousands of individuals and groups.

It's surprising how easily most people get in touch with their past lives. Since Soul Journeys therapy involves minds being fully engaged in the process, a person must be focused enough to stay with the experience, even when unpleasant material emerges. The art of doing Soul Journeys therapy involves navigating a client consciously through painful episodes to release the emotional charges contained in them. This is a process that requires specially trained therapists or health care practitioners.

When you do the following simplified version of a Soul Journey, it's important to trust whatever memories come to the surface without questioning or judging them or yourself. It may be challenging at first for some, but try to set aside your analytical mind for a while and observe the experience without criticizing what is happening or discounting your experience with the statement: It's only my imagination.

the past-life museum exercise

Begin this exercise by identifying a stubborn habit, fear, emotional blockage, or health issue that concerns you. These may be certain karmic patterns or dynamics, emotional overreactions, triggers, or hidden wounds you suspect are affecting your relationships.

Sitting or lying quietly with your eyes closed, breathe deeply and slowly for about a minute or two. Invite your spiritual guide, guardian angel, or inner teacher to assist you.

Now enter your own Past-Life Museum. It is usually seen with marble-like floors and pictures along the walls that depict your most significant past lives. Some may even see an occasional statue or sculpture. Notice how the floor appears, if there is any obvious pattern or color. Then look up toward the ceiling and notice how it appears. Then look around you at the general layout of the museum.

Now look for your teacher or spirit guide. Is he or she to your front, right, left, or rear? Ask your spiritual guide to direct your attention to the lifetime that has the greatest influence on whatever concern you identified. If you are unaware of your spirit guides, just know they are there and let your attention be naturally drawn to an image of the life having the greatest pull or energy for you.

Examine the image in your Past-Life Museum to which your attention is drawn or directed. If you like, begin to enter into this scene and review what was happening during this significant lifetime. It will play like a movie on your mind's screen or you will actually find yourself within the scene.

You may not see the entire life but after reviewing it's most significant segments, return to the museum. There, you may ask your guide questions about what you've experienced. When you feel complete, thank your guide. Gently move your attention back to your body in the present. Open your eyes.

soul journey enhancement

Prayer, meditation, and contemplation have always been powerful tools to expand the awareness and pierce the veil of consciousness when used properly. On occasion during Soul Journeys sessions, I use sound or mantras to further open the inner vision, and bring greater clarity to a past-life or between-life experience. It can also have a healing and cleansing effect after a session. This is accomplished by lightly singing, with the eyes closed, *hu* (pronounced like the name Hugh) on the outgoing breath just prior to entering into the Past Life Museum. *Hu* is an ancient and powerful mantra that has been used for centuries to bring greater alignment with the Soul. When necessary, you may lightly *hu* for 30 seconds or so during a Soul Journeys session to clarify details during the experience. Later, one can sing *hu* for longer periods to heal and balance the energies after reviewing past-life material. While doing this one can also look to whatever *Higher Power*, guide, or spiritual teacher they honor for inner direction.

after your visit to the past-life museum

With Soul Journeys sessions, you'll get what you ask for. I've found the Past-Life Museum exercise to be very powerful and precise. Using it may bring up strong emotions. You may want to speak with a skilled or sympathetic counselor, therapist, or spiritual advisor, so you can discuss what you experienced in a past life and the emotions that may have arisen from the memories. Remember that you may not gain access to certain traumatic past lives and have resulting therapeutic effects without the guidance of a trained Soul Journeys therapist.

Now is also the time, if you aren't already doing so, to begin a journal and record your Soul Journeys experiences. As you recall memories by doing the Past-Life Museum and other exercises in this book, look especially for events, stemming from past lives, which you're presently acting out. You may discover many of your actions and concerns today have been conditioned by past-life traumas or losses.

By taking time to reflect and write in your journal, you'll become more objective about your actions and begin to recognize the influence of past-life events. You'll also start to realize certain circumstances or people that trigger reactions rooted in past-life experiences. With this new awareness, you can change how you respond to situations.

future life possibilities

Although you will use the Past-Life Museum exercise to Soul Journey to previous incarnations, there are periods between lifetimes when you, as soul, prepare for what is to come. Just as people physically come together to accomplish certain tasks for learning and enjoyment, souls do the same thing in the between-life state. New incarnations are conceived and planned very much like a theater performance or play. Roles are chosen with the most suitable soul chosen to play a specific role, based on both positive and negative past-life karmic affinities.

Soul Groups are continually helping each other learn spiritual lessons as they work to balance some past karmic imbalances. Just as an actor will choose a role to expand his skill and stretch his range of expression, a soul will choose a lifetime to expand it's capacity for love and increase spiritual realization. This might even be done indirectly by choosing a lifetime of power and influence to learn how to handle power and influence.

There are also clients, who have been unconsciously afraid of their power, that have had lifetimes where they had great power and abused it. In these cases we have to go back to such a life, so they can consciously review the lifetime and forgive themselves. In so doing, they gain greater understanding and compassion for the past choices they made. This allows them to trust and accept themselves more in this life. In a past lifetime, when a soul abused power, could suggest the reasoning behind a person's fear of success in this lifetime.

After a Soul Group has decided on the respective roles each will play in an incarnation, there is a period of study and review.

In the between-life state, it's easy to see that the concept of time is only relative. This makes it possible for Soul Groups to ignore time constraints and preview a selected lifetime to come.

Two questions come to mind that I wonder if you're thinking right now. First, where does freedom of choice come into play if souls know the future beforehand? And, second, what is the value of knowing the future?

Just because a soul can preview a future life, doesn't mean that this is the only possible future. What the soul saw in the preview was just the most desired and preferred future, based on its present state of knowingness. The previewed future reflects the likely direction of that soul's present spiritual momentum. There are also other potential future projections that can be reviewed, but a soul chooses and focuses on the ideal one. This is the one it most hopes to realize.

The process of a soul previewing the future is like mentally rehearsing a performance of any kind. It could be in sports, dance, a play, an interview, or a speech. We can envision a certain ideal performance and outcome. The more we rehearse this ideal and the clearer it becomes in our imagination, the more likely it is that we will realize our goal. We also know that when the actual event occurs, we will likely forget our rehearsal, because we're fully absorbed in the moment. Yet we have already established a mental and emotional pattern of behavior that can more easily manifest, as we had hoped. This is the point where pre-destiny and choice come together.

the pre-life rehearsal exercise

If you'd like to remind yourself of this Pre-Life Rehearsal, try an exercise that might bring some of this information back to you. Next time you're anticipating an important event or performance, try doing mental rehearsals as a meditative experience. Get into the feeling of the event until your desired outcome becomes clear and natural. Many others and I have used this method with excellent results. As you did before you entered this life, you are the cause who is creating an effect. This exercise reminds you of the fact that you are either one or the other—cause or effect.

Which will it be for you?

Even though my clients are not hypnotized and they Soul Journey in full consciousness, the between-life state is not typically an area that they can gain easy access to without skilled guidance or many years of inner spiritual discipline. It will be beneficial for you to become aware of the between-life state because, as you are more attuned to your inner self, memories of it may flash into view during dreams or even while doing the Past-Life Museum Soul Journeys exercise.

In the next chapter we will begin to take a look at the karmic agreements souls make between-lives. We will explore the pre-life experiences souls have with friends, loved ones, teachers, and guides, and the wealth of understandings and insights available there.

In Chapter 11, the first entry into the between-life state is the focus of our exploration. There, you will have an opportunity to observe and understand many of the so-called mysteries that occur after death when loved ones, family, spiritual guides, and the karmic council all convene.

part 3

deep healing
invisible relationship wounds

Between-life Karmic Agreements

NOT MUCH HAS BEEN WRITTEN FROM AN EXPERIENTIAL PERSPECTIVE about what happens between-lives or how the between-life state and soul agreements made there affect relationships today. Certainly many people have had near-death experiences, and these have been well documented. But the experiences pushing past the period just after death and moving more directly into the other side still remain somewhat of a mystery.

I've heard a very competent regression therapist say that the only way to access the between-life state is through deep trance using hypnosis. In my practice I've found this to be untrue. As with past-life recall, my sessions have achieved Soul Journeys to the between-lives period with full conscious awareness.

Limits to your experience of reality are very often created by your own assumptions about what's possible and what's not. A principle in quantum physics states that an outcome is always influenced by the interaction between the subject and object. As a psychotherapist and facilitator of healing, I'm constantly in the process of challenging my own assumptions and beliefs. I don't want to influence the outcome of anyone's Soul Journeys in a limiting manner. So keeping myself open to all possibilities serves to minimize any limits or unwanted constraints I might inadvertently place on their experiences.

As a matter of spiritual respect, I have no interest in pushing anyone beyond his or her chosen belief or acceptance level. With this in mind, what I have found is that not all are ready for and receptive to having between-life Soul Journeys experiences. Such experiences can certainly challenge more traditional religious beliefs regarding life, death, and heaven. For this reason, only clients who express a genuine interest and desire to gain insight through this avenue do I guide through the between-life state.

Viewing the between-life state is certainly one of the best ways I've found to get an overview of your karmic agreements and love bonds with other souls, your goals for the present-life, lessons that brought you into this lifetime, and the teachers and guides who have been with you all along the way.

It's not unusual for someone to emerge from between-life experiences with tears of joy and gratitude at the beauty and magnificence of life and the spiritual journey. I can only be thankful to be a witness and facilitator of such experiences.

soul mates

During many of my clients' experiences in heavenly classrooms, they've reported that they were accompanied by souls that are in their Soul Group or are their soul mates. Over many lifetimes, certain groups of souls that have common interests, needs, and affinities, will come together and continue weaving in and out of each others' past and future lives, forming tight bonds of acceptance and love.

When I use the term soul mates, I'm defining it loosely to identify those souls you have formed a deep and abiding love bond with over many lifetimes. They include same and opposite sex individuals. Unlike the old soul mate theory that there is only one love of a lifetime for each person, I have not found evidence that there is one unique soul in the universe that you need to find and bond with to feel spiritually whole and content.

The soul mate theory is a distorted projection in the physical world of an inner transformation for spiritual wholeness that must eventually occur within each of us. It doesn't come to completion by merging with another soul. This inner transformation and completion of the soul involves balancing and integrating the male and female energies within one's self. It also includes integrating your Shadow with the persona—your more conscious self-expression. Actually Shadow integration must come before integration of the inner male or female.

Using past-life recall we can greatly accelerate the integration of the Shadow with the persona, and the inner masculine and feminine. The reason for this is because we are working in the literal instead of the symbolic realm with past lives. What this means is that you have a direct experience of your Shadow and inner male or female. The Shadow is expressed in past lifetimes when we have been a victimizer and abused power. The inner male and female manifest throughout past lives when one switches genders. What better way to integrate these parts of yourself than to experience them directly as you? The symbolic interpretation and realization is valuable but it's still conceptual and one step removed from your direct literal experience.

what's waiting for you in between-lives

Moving into the between-life state usually begins with a review of the most recent life prior to your present one. Even though time is relative in these realms, it does provide a mental construct for the conscious mind to more easily transition from a past life to between-lives on the other side.

From both my professional practice and years of personal spiritual experiences, I've come to know that everyone dies and reincarnates. Between incarnations, even though we've dropped the physical body, the soul and other energetic forms of ourselves, such as the mind and emotions, live in a state that can be labeled "heaven." You might be surprised to know this isn't the traditional place of clouds, harps, and eternal bliss. Instead, the between-life state offers souls the opportunity to rest up and repair from their most previous incarnation and prepare for their next one. I've found this preparation can be somewhat basic or quite extensive depending on the soul or souls involved. There, as here, different individuals plan and function at different levels.

By way of example we will follow the experience of a happily married woman named Joan. Within the transcript of her Soul Journeys session, I'll make some comments to help explain what Joan is seeing or how it might apply to your life.

Joan is a mother and grandmother in her mid-fifties, full bodied, with a very joyful and engaging presence. She came to me because of challenges with authority she'd had in her life and was experiencing currently with her boss at the bank where she worked. Joan also had other minor fears we addressed during her sessions, such as the fear of swimming underwater, or being held down or restrained.

We had been through several past-life Soul Journeys to resolve Joan's difficulties and fears. In her next session we transitioned into a between-life period she'd had prior to this lifetime for greater insight into the choices she had made that were affecting her relationships and life today. After reviewing the trauma of an Egyptian lifetime to resolve Joan's fear of being underwater, I guided her into the afterlife, or between-life state, to get further insight. This is what she recounted.

Joan's Between-Life Memories

C: Be outside of the body after that Egyptian life and describe what you experienced.

J: Suddenly I feel like a rush of wind and I move upward fast. I am attracted to beams of light that seem to come from above. They are warm, and I move up along one of them and see brightness below me. I am surrounded by brightness.

C: What do you see around you?

J: I am standing on the edge of a bright space and see people and animals. It is a white city built on a hill. I walk into it on one of the streets. These are wide streets lined with houses that are attached on either side. I walk on and get to the end and see a park with green grass and water.

C: Describe the general layout of the city as you see it.

J: The entire city is built on a slope that goes up to a plateau and forms a huge park. It is built like a hub with the streets as the spokes. There are people, but they appear like wisps. It is very busy, and everybody is coming and going with lots of activity. I look around and am alone.

C: Continue and describe what you do next.

J: I know there is a Visitors Center. I keep moving toward a huge open building with walls. I wait for someone to tell me where I am supposed to go.

With more advanced souls after death, there is an immediate recognition of where they are and what needs to be done. This is because you've been through the process numerous times before. It's like coming back to your hometown after many years. Certain things may have changed or been modified, but it still feels familiar and generally you know your way around.

C: What do you see next?

J: An old man is there. I know him. He has the appearance of a physical form but it keeps shifting. He shows me the different ways he looked physically when I knew him. He stands at the bottom of steps. He welcomes me as he shows me who he has been, so I will recognize him. As he waits for me, he says, "Hurry up," but he's not impatient. He is glad to see me, and I am glad to see him. I throw my arms around him.

C: How does he appear to you now?

J: He wears flowing white clothes. They look white because it is so bright. I want to call him grandfather, because in my previous life he was my grandfather. He says, "Come along. I have things to show you."

C: Often the first soul or souls that greet you when you transition into the between-life state are loved ones. This is done for obvious reasons. Some souls may not be fully aware when their body first dies and they need a loved and trusted guide to help orient them. This is especially the case when there has been a traumatic or sudden death. Souls, that greet you, are often those with whom you've had karmic ties.

Meeting Soul Groups

C: What do you experience next?

J: We are at the front of an open building. Then we proceed down a hall with lots of different rooms on either side. The rooms are not really defined by walls, and I want to stick my head in them, but he says, "No, we need to start at the beginning." We get to the end of a hallway, and we go into a room where there are lots of people.

C: Describe the room you are in.

J: The room is circular, but I don't have the sense of being in a room. Other people are there, and we know each other. Lots of love flows back and forth between everybody. We settle down and all sit cross-legged. My grandfather is in the front. It is almost like a class, and he is the teacher.

C: What does the teacher do next?

J: He asks us to go one by one and introduce ourselves. To say who we are and why we are there. Nobody wants to go first.

C: How are you positioned in the room?

J: He is sitting on nothing yet is elevated. We are relaxed. I sit cross-legged with my elbow on my knee and chin in my hand. It's like we are sort of hanging in space.

C: Now what are you doing?

J: I'm looking at more than one of my lifetimes as images quickly flash across my vision. I consider with this how I am to introduce myself. We have all shared lifetimes together. I look at another person I sense is female. I did not know her in my last lifetime, so now she is someone different to me, and I am someone different to her.

In the between-life state after a physical incarnation, souls will often maintain the general form of their most recent lifetime for a time. Because of this, if it's been many lifetimes since you've seen a familiar soul, you may not recognize exactly who it is at first. Additionally, if they've been in the between-life state for a while, any "physical" form the soul may take will seem indistinct unless necessity dictates otherwise. This was the case with the soul Joan sensed was a female from one of her past lives.

Souls, in the between-life state can assume any form they choose. For this reason they may assume or project a familiar form merely for convenience sake.

C: Continue.

J: I introduce myself to each person in terms of the lifetime we shared together.

C: How many of you are in the room?

J: There are about 12 of us. The first person I see was my sister in another life. I was male. She has a headband and a long, dark braid. We shared a life together as Native Americans. I appear to her with long black hair—tall, thin, and muscular. She is tall and lean. Certain images of that life come. We lived in a green area with trees, mountains, streams, and lakes. As children, we did lots together with much freedom.

C: What are the others in the room doing?

J: Everyone else in the room is doing the same thing with each other.
      The two of us turn to another person who was our playmate in that lifetime. As we notice each other, we are into that lifetime. We show ourselves as children. The other person is male. He became my sister's husband. I hunted with him.

In that lifetime our teacher here in the class was an important teacher for us as children. We turn to him and now see him as he was in that lifetime. He is an elder with long, flowing, gray hair. He is lean with dark, piercing eyes. Very kind and loving. [Joan tears up, sighs, and has a revelation.] The old Indian is my mother in this present lifetime. We want to stay where we were in that Indian lifetime, because we all felt lots of love then.

C: Do you know anyone else in the room?

J: Yes, we are all connected from previous lifetimes, some more directly than others. Another person here that I look to is a female, blonde with blue eyes and very fair skin. She wears a bright-blue fancy dress. It is not how I have known her in a past life, but how I may come to know her. We have shifted to a future time track. I am having trouble keeping the time track straight. I am a little confused, and she is laughing.

C: Time in the between-life state is more fluid, and souls can move forward or backward on the time track. This allows them to preview a possible future life or a past life in the physical world at will. I use the word "possible future life" because the future is not fixed in stone and there are many possibilities. We all have freedom of choice from moment to moment but our state of consciousness and fluidity of awareness determines our future direction.

It's like using physics to predict the movement of an object in space based on its current momentum. Such predictions can be quite accurate when accounting for all obvious variables. However, the influence of soul can change the variables in an instant. Soul is like the "wild card." Because of this, the more consciously soul-directed you are, the more options or future possibilities are available for your choosing. More conscious freedom means less predictability.

Future Lives Become Clearer

C: How do you see the girl in the blue dress?

J: We are not old. We are like 20 or so. Female. We are talking in a large garden. She's laughing because she has continually played tricks on me. It's like a game. The teacher says, "Now get serious." She calms down and gets serious, but is showing me so many lives at one time that it's confusing. We have lived lots of lives together as friends, brother and sister, with lots of love. This is why she is feeling so playful. She has been here longer than I have and has already made some choices about her next life.

C: You were to be in her future lifetime?

J: She is trying to coax my interest in the lifetime she has selected. Showing me how it could be for both of us there.
   The old man is laughing because he would be with us in that lifetime also. He's thinking, "Well, we will see."

C: What are the others doing?

J: We are all getting to know each other again. The circle widens as we share lifetimes, but soon it will get real serious. I need to know who I was and why I had to live that last lifetime. Following the timeline gets really hard. I want to understand why I was a slave in that Egyptian lifetime. I know that I died, because there was nothing more to be learned.

Teachers and Classes

C: What was behind your choice of that lifetime?

J: I chose it to learn humility. By experiencing humility as a slave, I learned not to force my will on other people. In previous lives I had been pretty arrogant and domineering. In the lifetime I shared with the first girl, I was a hunter and warrior. I had lots of stature and was not very tolerant. As an Egyptian galley slave, I managed to hold onto the idea that I was learning humility.

C: Anything else about your owners on the galley slave ship?

J: My owners in that life were dark-skinned Egyptians.

C: What is the purpose of your gathering there with the others?

J: We are all trying to bring into the present consciousness all those insights and lessons about the recent life, so when we meet the teacher, we can focus on all the things we learned and still need to learn.

We are going to a lot of different classes to learn more about the spiritual and physical laws before we go into another life. The teacher says that part of the learning is having experiences that show us whether we learned certain principles of life. We'll see how many times we have studied this before, prior to previous lives, and did not get the lesson during the next lifetime.

> The teacher takes us through lots of phases. As time goes on, we might break up into smaller groups.

Classes in the between-life state are common for souls. Preparation for a future life and the lessons we incarnate to learn are first taught to us within the various classes. These classes are even available during a physical incarnation in the dream state if soul has the awareness and desire to visit them. The between-life state shows us that there is a lesson to be learned in whatever situation you find yourself in during your life in the physical body. Taking a moment to reflect on this when challenging situations come up, can bring awareness of the lesson to consciousness.

C: What is the teacher's name?

J: He is Yoseph. We regard him as a teacher or master.

C: How do you appear to one another, generally?

J: We see each other the way that we knew each other in the lifetime when we were together. We are still somewhat identified with the physical world and bodies we had then.

C: What kind of meeting are you in?

J: This is an orientation class at say, a graduate level, instead of a high school or college level. I could bypass the earlier steps.

C: Are there any colors involved in your appearance?

J: Yes, we radiate colors—mostly blue. I look like a mostly blue rainbow.

C: How about Yoseph, the master?

J: The master radiates more of a brightness than a color. He is light blue going into white and is so bright that I can see through him.

Joan's Egyptian past life

C: Let's go back to your previous life in Egypt as a galley slave. Be there now and tell me, were you always at sea?

J: No, at times we are on the river. I think it is the Nile. Most everyday is spent on the water. Our owner would bring his family on the boat for pleasure. There are 12 to 14 of us slaves on his private ship. It is a smaller, light ship. He races us against his friends. He is very proud of us, as we are very fast.

    At a certain point, I am too old and don't have the endurance. He sells or trades me to a much larger ship.

C: How large?

J: Maybe 25 or 30 slaves are manning the oars on this ship at once. We travel longer distances and row in shifts. We are chained. A violent storm swamps the ship, and it takes on too much water. The ship carries cargo, and we cross long distances. There is a deck above that protects us from exposure. Also, they load the upper deck with cargo.

C: What was the crew like?

J: I am dark-skinned but not all of the slaves are of that coloring. There are all degrees of color from dark to white. One or two have red hair. Some are being punished as criminals, and it is either life as a slave or death.

C: What about the owners?

J: The owners are white. I never see their families.

C: What was your life like on this ship?

J: Your only value is your strength and health. If you get sick, they throw you overboard to save the weight.

C: Where did you travel?

J: The ship sails down a very large river that empties into the sea.

C: What continent?

J: It is my continent, Africa.

C: What about your ship, how did it appear?

J: Which one?

C: The first one that was smaller.

J: The boat is really beautiful, and the colors are very bright. A large symbol of the sun in gold is on the boat.

C: What about the larger boat?

J: The second boat is only ocean going, and the owners are not Egyptian. They are taller in stature and have lighter skin and hair. They trade with the Egyptians. I am sold to them from Egypt.

C: Were you at sea day and night?

J: When we are not on the river, we spend time in our quarters on the property. We are confined to a certain space, but our living quarters are fairly open, and the weather is mild.

C: What were the quarters like?

J: They are made of clay and thatched woven grass. Some wood in the frame but not a lot. Mostly clay bricks and grass.

     The Egyptians tend to paint their buildings in color. It is out in the country and has a rich reddish color.

     I have been raised as a galley slave and am a child of a slave. I do not understand the bitterness and anger of the others on the larger ship because of my upbringing.

As you can see, during the between-life state soul can review a past-life segment as easily as watching a video clip. This is where time collapses in the now. All is available in the present moment. In her original between-life experience, it's unlikely that Joan cut to the Egyptian past life as I asked her to do during our session. This is like changing past events while you are in the present, which will also influence the future. All Soul Journeys sessions into past events have the effect of changing the past, present, and future, because these time designations only exist in the mind. Soul lives in the eternal now.

In that Egyptian past life Joan is born to be subservient to authority in a role that requires a degree of humility to survive without bitterness.

Past-Life Movies

C: Be back at your orientation meeting after that life. What do you do next?

J: The master ends the meeting and gives us free time to interact. We continue to talk, tease, argue, and discuss different aspects of past lives we have shared. It is ongoing because we all have done things to one another we wish we hadn't done.

C: How do you see these lifetimes?

J: It is like we are watching segments of movies we project to review and compare.

C: Compared to what?

J: We compare other lives to our most recent life. We are learning to relate it all back to the principles and spiritual laws we are trying to learn. We recognize where we had fallen short and then got it and did it right. We all have something to teach each other.

C: This idea of examining the success of your application of the spiritual principles is one you can also use during your present-life here. I will often review a situation I've experienced to determine if I used love or power, a creative or a reactive response. If any unconscious fear contaminated my action, I might consider it's source and what would be a more ideal expression of soul in such a situation.

Again, this is a way of reviewing the past to change the present and future all in the now.

C: What is your next meeting like?

J: The next major meeting is with a teacher who is not necessarily our teacher. I meet first with a woman who appears quite young. She is a teacher with blonde hair and is dressed in soft blue.

C: Where are you located?

J: The setting is off a ways but in the same structure. It is a smaller, quieter area.

C: What is the purpose of this meeting?

J: To look at my most recent life and why I choose that life and to help me look at whether I feel that I had accomplished what I had set out to accomplish. From there, I would go to the group again for more general classes.

having the between-life state now

Joan's experience is typical of the initial stages of review after a physical incarnation. However, there are infinite variations in how this is experienced by different souls. The differences are based on the beliefs, awareness, expectations, and past-life history of each individual soul. Souls from various religious faiths or beliefs will experience variations that reflect the way different groups handle the between-life state. Certainly all the between-life experiences go way beyond our commonly accepted notions of the afterlife but again, each set of Soul Groups has its own protocols.

When you meet someone from your Soul Group, you are going to find this person familiar right away. There is a natural ease and understanding between you that has to do with your shared love and spiritual resonance as souls. When I meet someone new, I often ask the soul within: What is the larger purpose of our meeting? Is it friendship, romance, business or creative project, a karmic resolution, teaching exchange, a soul companion, or some combination of the above? Sometimes it can be just a brief sharing of love and understanding along the journey. Conversely, it's also necessary at times to ask if a cycle has completed with a certain individual or group and it's time to move on.

These are all questions we know or have known before birth but have forgotten. Consciously inviting that soul awareness is a step that can reopen the doors to spiritual insight. It's important to remember that all life is a spiritual experience in varied guises. Here, as in the between-life state, it helps tremendously if you interact frequently with souls who share that understanding.

In Chapter 12, we will continue with Joan's between-life experiences. During this section we get to see many of the factors that go into Joan's choice of her current lifetime as a joyful and loving mother and grandmother. Her experiences may help you understand more about how the between-life state, with its classrooms, teachers and reflection time, have influenced your choices in life and your relationships.

chapter 12

Choosing This Lifetime

On occasion I hear seekers or those involved with spiritual studies say, "I chose this lifetime," or "I chose my family." Certainly, I've found much truth to such claims, but considering how we respond to our chosen life on some occasions, I consider how easily we forget.

Another thing I sometimes hear is, "This is my last incarnation on earth." This would certainly be desirable for many, but my observation is that once soul has reached a stage where it could choose not to reincarnate, it's more likely to just say, "Thy will be done," and is no longer attached to the time or place of it's next lifetime.

Until we've met all the requirements and passed the last test, our graduation from the wheel of physical incarnation is unconfirmed.

It's also apparent that certain choices of embodiment that seem challenging or lacking in specific areas such as finance, education, or even appearance may result in greater spiritual gains in a particular lifetime than a so-called charmed life. It's all about the heart. What seems desirable here in our society may not be such an advantage in the spiritual sense. Even though everything can be considered a spiritual experience, our choices from lifetime to lifetime depend on what we're here to learn.

With this mission of learning in mind, we'll explore some questions you may have about choosing a lifetime: What's involved when a soul chooses to return to a physical embodiment from the between-life state? Is this actually a choice a soul can make? What other decisions go into forming and shaping the incarnation to come?

The process of choosing to return to life on earth is somewhat different for each I've worked with. As mentioned in the previous chapter, these differences are largely determined by background, belief, past-life history, temperament, and of course, level of spiritual awareness. A soul with a passion for music but little interest in religion may choose a family that is naturally musical but noncommittal when it comes to religion. Certain karmic affinities between souls involving music, science, politics, law, sports, and many other interests can determine the choice of certain lifetimes.

In the last chapter you met Joan, who had a Soul Journey to the between-life state. As we continue with Joan's transcript, it resumes with a lifetime just prior to her present one. Her example and the commentaries I'll make on it should give you more perspective on what happens as a soul prepares to move from one incarnation to the next incarnation. Joan's recollections may also give you insights on how to make better spiritual use of the choices you made long ago.

If you've ever wondered what happens when you die, what heaven is like, or how souls make the journey from one life to the next, Joan's story offers startling revelations.

Death and Dying

C: Are you sitting, standing, or lying?

J: I am a fit, well-built, male warrior. I am standing outdoors where I view unbeliev- able carnage. I am filled with rage, despair, horror, and heartbreak because this is my

village. I look to find anyone alive. This is
slaughter. I've been in battle many times
before, and it was terrifying because of the
people who were killed. This is senseless.

C: How do you appear physically?

J: I am a brown-skinned Native American.
I see tepees nearby.

C: What started the battle?

J: We were trying to defend our land. We are
basically peaceful and only hunt for food. We
have been pushed back and pursued too far.
When the council decided to confront our
enemy, we never dreamed we would be
slaughtered.

C: Did another tribe attack you?

J: We were attacked by soldiers, not another
tribe. Before the soldiers came, the land
was so vast; we did not need to fight one
another. We respected our land and each
other. The tribes only fought with each other
as the soldiers pushed us back. We did not
understand the ways of the soldiers. At first,
we fought among ourselves but then we
stopped quickly. The way they slaughtered
us broke our spirit. I have a great sadness
and realize it is something that can't be
stopped.

C: How does your life continue from there?

J: We try to move to safe places, but there is
no rest. I am growing old. Gradually we are
confined. It is a sad life. My grandchildren
will not grow to be a part of the land, and
I am brokenhearted. I live a long life until my
fifties, and my hair is white. I have become
a storyteller and try to keep alive the history—
try to teach the young ones.

C: How does that lifetime end for you?

J: It is cold. I am sick and I just kind of let go. I decide it is time and refuse the herbs and normal tribal remedies. My wounds from battle have crippled me somewhat.

C: What tribe do you belong to?

J: We are part of the Sioux Nation. I die quietly in the winter. I have been positioned to lie on my back. They have dressed me in my head-dress and painted my face in war paint.

moving out of the body at death

The process of moving out of the body after death is quite natural for the many taken through this process during a Soul Journey. Often the soul wants to be outside of the body even before it has completely expired. After death some souls may stay on earth for a period of time, but most leave immediately after a brief overview of their surroundings. The reason some souls may stay for a period of time can vary from love attachments to confusion, anger, shame, or even to try and influence unfinished business.

C: As you move up and outside of the body upon dying, what do you see?

J: I can see that they have prepared a burial place. I still feel very sad. As I look toward the sky, it starts to get brighter.

C: What do you notice there?

J: I feel very alone at first. As I move forward and toward the brightness, Yoseph is there.

You may recall that Yoseph is Joan's spiritual guide from Chapter 11 and also was her grandfather in a previous lifetime.

C: Where do you see him?

J: He is in the distance, but I can see him in the light. He is holding his hand out. [Joan begins to sob lightly.]

C: How does he appear?

J: He is smiling. He looks like an Indian Chief. He wears a long headdress that goes all the way down to the ground. And he is telling me not to be sad. I'm not afraid but I still have sadness as I reach him. He takes me by the hand. We are walking but we are not walking. We just move through what appears at first to be clouds and later, look like colors.

C: What colors?

J: Unbelievable colors. Golds and blues. Everything is so vivid. It's like a kaleidoscope. We are moving through these colors, and they are liquid. It is as if they are washing and healing the sadness.

C: What is he saying?

J: He's saying, "Remember. Remember that this was just one life, and it is not really where you live." He is telling me that he is thinking thoughts. I can hear his thoughts. He is saying, "You know the way. You've been this way before. We are going to go home now. You need to rest for awhile."

C: Where does he take you?

J: We go through all these colors, and then he asks me where I want to rest. I choose a place that looks like the land I just left. I want to sit by the lake and that's okay, that's okay. He says that he has things to do but he'll be back. So I sit cross-legged by the lake and sing to myself because I am not quite ready to let go.

As the peacefulness settles within me, Yoseph is back. We move away and now we are starting to move very fast. He asks, "Are you ready?"

And I say, "Yes, I'm ready. Let's get on with it. Now I'm eager."

C: Are you still in the same form?

J: I am gradually fading, as far as the physical form. I have a physical form of sorts, but as we move faster, we don't have as much substance and are becoming almost transparent. We are moving very fast.

C: What are you seeing as you move?

J: At first, as we pass through the colors, I see places that are very much like where I lived on earth. Then, they start to fade. Before, I would have wanted to stay in these places, because they were comfortable. But now, I don't need to do that and am ready to move on.

Again, we are moving pretty fast, and mostly I am aware of the sound and colors. But I'm impatient. Yoseph is kind of teasing me. He says for someone that hung on as long as I did, once I made up my mind, I sure wanted to get back home.

C: What kind of sound do you hear?

J: It's like the roar of the ocean as we are moving. It starts to slow down, and Yoseph is telling me that the others are there. We can have some time to . . . it's funny, because he says play. "You can play now for awhile, but then we are going to get serious.'

Reunions

Almost without exception, my clients experience reunions with loved ones in the between-life state. There have even been occasions when, after death, their Soul Groups hold what appears to be a party in their honor. When a lifetime has been particularly traumatic or painful, the soul may choose to heal and recover by taking a rest at the start of the between-life experience.

C: Where do you finally arrive?

J: It is kind of like we are suspended. I can sense others around me. They are like blinking lights.

C: Any particular color?

J: Blue and some with a little purplish tinge, and others more towards white. They are almost playing tag, because they will come up and say, "Do you remember me?" Then they will flash so many images at me, since we have all had so many different appearances in previous lives. They are teasing me. It is really a happy time.

C: Do you notice being in any structures?

J: I am not aware initially of being in any structure, but there is a sense of being outside rather than inside. It is kind of like, as a group, if we decide that we want to be in the mountains, by a lake, or in a meadow, we can decide, and then it is just there. It is whatever we think we can enjoy. Then we just play. We laugh and talk. As I recognize each one, there is this wonderful feeling of love.

C: How many of you are there?

J: Six, maybe seven. There are not many of us at that time. Yoseph is letting me kind of relax and get used to being free of the physical body again. Between-lives, we realize we had this experience and that experience, except the experience was a whole lifetime.

The Life Review

The whole concept of a judgment day after death is woven throughout certain religions. It's even been depicted in various movies, but never have I read about the detailed experiences involving life reviews I've observed with those who have come to me. Again, certain specifics involving these experiences and the council, which conducts the life review, will vary from soul to soul, but their overall purpose remains constant. That purpose is to objectively review with the soul the previous life and determine the ideal options for a new incarnation.

J: Yoseph lets me enjoy for a while and then he comes back. He says, "Okay, lets think about what you have learned in this last experience."

C: Is he speaking to the whole group?

J: No, he is speaking right now to me. We are kind of off to one side. We have gone into what looks like a small pavilion and we sit at a table. If I were in physical form, I would probably have my chin in my hands. I'm not real eager to get down to business, but we do.

C: What are you discussing?

J: The love that I learned to have for my people, the land, and the animals. And even though I knew that death wasn't permanent, it was

hard for me to deal with the physical manifestation of dying. I'm telling him thatI don't want
to go through that again. Please, can I be
done with that?

C: What does Yoseph say?

J: He says, "Yes, you can." But I had been a
warrior in other lifetimes, and he shows
me scenes where I was very brutal. He says,
"You had to learn the other side of it to be
free of it." And also I had to learn how to
love, particularly the youngsters. That was part
of being of service—loving and nurturing.

C: What happens next?

J: We are looking at other lives, but in a general
way.

C: What kind of lives are you looking at?

J: First, he says that the life I just came from was
a very simple life. It wasn't real complicated. It
was chosen deliberately so I could not only
work off karma but also learn respect and
beauty, because these are a reflection of the
soul.
      He is very gentle and not critical. [He
shows scenes from a much earlier lifetime.]
He says, "See in this lifetime, you were very
selfish and defiant. In other lifetimes you
were very brutal." I have managed little by
little to let go of the hate and physical self-
ishness of wanting my way and wanting
things.

As you can see, in the between-life state Joan is shown
segments of previous lives as teaching tools regarding her
spiritual progress from life to life. In this state I've found
souls have easy access to the full range of their past-life
experiences.

C: How does Yoseph show you these lives? How do you see them?

J: He'll show me how I was and he'll say, "Do you remember when you did this or said that?" I'll see myself either as a female and dressed like I was—in a long, blue dress. It's a very quick image. Just so I can focus in.

We spend quite a bit of time looking at, "What do you think you've learned? Or did you learn?" It's like a thought process of my past life. "Before you thought you had to have this and had to have that, but in your last life you didn't have those things. Did you miss them in this life?" And I say, no. He tells me we are going to spend a bit of time looking at different things in past lives to decide about the next life. [Joan laughs.]

He tells me, "Really, this life [the one I just came out of], you know, was a pretty easy life." And I laugh at him. I think that's pretty funny. Because I didn't think it was easy at the time. He says, "Yes, you'll find out. The next one is not going to be quite so easy. You are going to have to work harder." He teases me and says, "You tend to be lazy."

As you may have realized by now, in life and relationships it takes greater effort for a soul to assert itself with love and creativity as opposed to negativity and habit. In the short run it's easier to remain unconscious, letting the mind and emotions continue in familiar patterns. When this happens, the soul has succumbed to the inertia of physical life and the greater pull of limitation experienced here on earth. The payoff for living life consciously and with passion is well worth the effort.

C:　What does he do with you next?

J:　He has somewhere else to go because he has other souls he's responsible for. So he tells me we are going to go back to the others.

C:　How does he appear, as you sit with him?

J:　Initially when he first met me this time, he appeared as a very old wise Indian chief. But as we moved through the different worlds, neither one of us had any form. Then as we slowed down, we could take any form we wanted. When he's teasing, the image that he'll pass to me is one of a young man. When we get more serious, he appears as older, and his eyes are so wise. He does this because he says, "You tend to think that you know it all." So he will flash an image to me that will make me see him as older and wiser. Which I know really that he is. And I have a lot to think about.

Reviewing Karmic Relationships

There are times when souls with deep and comfortable love bonds, which span many lives, may be separated in life to allow for karmic resolutions with other souls that are more challenging or painful. For some souls this separation may happen earlier in life, causing family members or loved ones to be separated or later in life, through loss or other factors. At the time it may seem a terrible loss, but it serves to temper soul and stimulate it to realize greater spiritual potential.

C:　What happens when you rejoin the other group?

J:　When we're all together with the ones we have been close to, we review the lives we've had together. We share with each other some of the lives in which maybe we were not closely associated. We might have been in the physical at the same time, but for whatever reason, we were not closely connected. We try to help each other see and understand better. Such as, "This is how this affected me or how I reacted to that." Sometimes it's, "Boy, was I stupid and I don't want to even think about that because I shouldn't have done that." And other times it's like, "Wow, I got that one right."

C: What is the basic purpose?

J: It's all learning. We all want to learn. We don't want to have to lose ground, as it were. We all have this real determination to bring forward. We know we are going to have to go into another life. We are not real thrilled about it because we like where we are. It is peaceful.

C: How do you know you will have to go into another life?

J: We know it because we have been through it before. It is the whole purpose of looking and reviewing like this. We have the feeling that we want to learn as much as we can and take as much back with us so we can start off, like, ahead of it.

C: Is it ever that you don't want to go back at all? That you have a choice?

J: Not at this time. We have a choice about how soon. But we know that once we've reviewed and learned what we need to learn, then we are going to have to start preparing to go into the next life. Right now, we want to learn but we are in a way, dragging our heels. We want to enjoy the freedom that we have. We are surrounded by love, light, and peace. There is laughter and there is joy here.

Meeting with the Council

C: How do you prepare next?

J: There are three or four guides who are eval-
uating and pointing out things that we don't
want to see, but that we need to see.

C: Whom do you meet with after Yoseph?

J: It is like a board or council. Yoseph tells me
it is time for me to go and talk with them.
Their purpose is to evaluate, but it is really
not like a judgment.

C: What are the surroundings like?

J: It is like a pavilion or temple. They are at a
table, and I sit down in front of them.

C: How are they positioned?

J: They sit in a row. I know them. It is kind of
like, "Welcome back."

C: How do they appear?

J: [She pauses.] Very light. There is light, love,
and gentleness.

C: Do they have any kind of form?

J: Only what I give them. They let me see them
as I want to. I tend to see them as older wise
men at this time, except two are female. We
exchange ideas and at first, it is kind of general. They are looking at what experiences
I need to have.

   They have a ledger and are looking at
my karma. What debts are still there that
need to be worked out? We are talking also,
and they are asking me what do I want to
concentrate on? It is like making an outline
that is general at first. Then the karma gets
down to specifics—other people, other souls
with whom I have debts I need to pay. And

then also, I am going to be allowed to
choose some things that I want to work on.

As you can see, the limits regarding your choice of a new incarnation are based on the debts you carry forward from previous lives. It's also the case that the credits you carry forward give you more options and opportunities to choose from. These choices have been described as "all fitting together like precise clockwork" by one client.

C: How is all of this communicated to you?

J: It is a thought process. Some thoughts are transmitted with visual images. It's like looking at a ledger and checking things off; determining that we need to include these specific things.

C: Do they all communicate to you at once?

J: They will confer with each other at certain points. Then there is the main one with whom I seem to talk. Occasionally, the others might ask questions or make a comment.

C: Is the one you communicate with the most a male or female?

J: It's a male. I see him as being older and wiser. A little bit of a higher stature than the others. They are all pretty equal, really. And they have studied. They have trained to do what they do. They are there to help each soul participate in planning its next lifetime. They are very careful not to let me take on too much.

C: How is it determined how much you take on?

J: We have all agreed that there is some substantial karma that I want to get out of the way. There are two parts of it. First, there is the karma. And beyond that, there are lessons I can choose to work on, like, love.

C: What do you choose then?

J: I choose love.

It's important to know that at any point in your current life or relationship you can ask to learn more about a specific virtue. In doing so you allow soul to have a more conscious influence in your life. In fact, you may have even planned before this lifetime to be more inspired by soul at this stage in your life. Life has many windows of opportunity that are either accepted or passed over.

C: What's your karma?

J: I know that I've been pretty nasty to some people. But I don't get a lot of input as to how to work it out. I know that I am going to have to meet these people again, and we are going to try to work it out. It is never just one-sided. But this council doesn't tell me a lot. Since I said that I want to work on love, meeting these people I've wronged again is the way I am going to have to work through the karma. By trying to be loving and taking responsibility.

    We have to decide in a general sense first, before we go on. I start by looking at a big picture. Then it narrows down to where I am looking at three or four family and life situations that I could go into.

Making Specific Choices

Have you ever considered that the life you have chosen is not based on the luck of the draw or blind fate? As you read on, you will see that your life circumstance is a choice you've earned and is carefully determined beforehand for its advantages and challenges.

C: How do you see those life situations you could choose?

J: I am shown them like a motion picture. I look above the heads of the council members. They say, "If you choose to be male, go into this body." It is just like an outline. Then we get down to the type of body, whether it will be a healthy body, a taller body, whatever. And they show me several vignettes along the way regarding how that life is going to progress. These are things like the body I am going to inhabit, when I will be born, and the family I am going to be born into. Also, the circumstances that family will be in. I don't want to be a male again. I want to come into a female body.

C: Why do you decide you don't want to be a male?

J: Because I feel it would be easier in a female body to express love and a loving nature and to show compassion.

C: Other than that reason, it doesn't matter to you whether it is male or female?

J: No it doesn't seem to. It's just that in looking at the lifetimes I can choose, I feel that, as a female, I can better develop the part of myself I want to improve.

C: There is no particular attachment or preference to being male or female, even though you have just come from a male body?

J: I kind of don't want to be male again because I got beat up physically. All around, I want a gentler type of life. I am thinking initially that I would have less responsibility as a female. It doesn't work out that way, but that is what I am thinking in that mental part of me.

C: Have you ever chosen to be gay in a lifetime?

J: I've had lifetimes where it didn't really matter. The sexes intermingled: female-to-female, female-to-male, and male-to-male. There were times when, in the pursuit of the sexual, it didn't make any difference. That seemed like it was a long time ago.

Choosing the Parents

C: Once you decide on a female body, what next?

J: I know that once in the physical body, it is difficult for a soul to keep the compass straight, so to speak. So choosing my mother is real important. And this is when I first think that I wish Yoseph could be there to guide me. And I am not quite sure how it will come about, whether he will actually be my mother or whether he will be there to guide her.

At this point, I am seeing Yoseph and my mother as one and the same. They are to teach me love—unconditional love. This is a real important decision. I want Yoseph as my mother so bad that the council sees this would be the best situation. And I know that Yoseph is not going to be on the physical plane with me for much time. It will be limited, but it will be enough.

C: Are you still with the council?

J: Yes, but we take breaks. We look at the premise. Then the next time we meet, they show me two or three different lives. I will not necessarily have full choice of which one is going to best fit what has been decided upon. Next time I see them, it's like a movie or a show for me.

Life Maps

C.   What do you do between times after the
     premise has been established?

J: I go back to my friends, and we talk. We are at
     different parts of the process. Some of them
     have been there longer and are involved in
     more direct preparation to go back into the
     lifetime they are going to go into.
          Once a decision is made, it is not like,
     boom, you go into that. You are looking at
     it and deciding choices and directions. My
     friends are trying to explain to me that you
     have to know the cycles. It's like a map, and
     you have to know what direction to go.
     There are different things that you are going
     to be briefed on so when you are back in that
     lifetime, hopefully you will recognize on the
     soul level that you are supposed to go this
     way or that way.

Often upon hearing about or seeing a certain person or
situation in life, you are compelled to act in a specific way.
That will-to-action, when inspired by the heart, is an
impulse from soul.

C: Getting back to your decision. The others tell
     you there will be signposts to recognize?

J: You decide on your map or how you want to
     live this life ideally. But you know that once
     you get back into the physical world and
     body, you will forget. Each of us gets a chance
     to study ahead of time, the life that we are
     going to go into.

C: Is this after your first review?

J: Yes, because it starts general and it gets spe-
     cific and definite, once the particular body

and life is determined—that you are going to be born to this mother in these circumstances.

The Second Review

C: What about the second review?

J: Yoseph comes to get me, and we go back to the council. It is like we are in a schoolroom, yet each one of us is only seeing what we need in terms of the life we are going back to. It's like there is a teacher or one of the guides, and they are pointing out scenes, like seeing a motion picture. They show, for instance, that at this point, you need to know this. And you can determine what your cues will be.

C: What do you decide to notice there about this lifetime?

J: In picking my first husband, that he is kind to me. I am focusing on the first time I have any-thing to do with him. He is helping me with scheduling my classes and he doesn't have to do this.

As with Joan's experience above, these cues may be any observation, exchange, or action that makes you take notice or that seems out of the ordinary.

C: How do you see the situation with your husband in the review?

J: I actually see the situation like a movie.

This could account for the déjà vu many people occa-sionally experience in life.

C.: You are in a classroom with other souls?

J: Yes, and it's weird because there are a lot of us together, but we are each seeing our own lives. It's like being in a big theater with a whole bunch of different screens.

C: One teacher is directing it all?

J: Yes, that is what is so strange about it. Your attention gets directed and you are left to focus on that, while the teacher works with somebody else. And it is just one teacher. Strange way they do it.

C: How does this teacher appear to you?

J: [She laughs.] Really about all I see is like a pointer. The teacher points to whatever you are supposed to be directing your attention to. I think it is a female.

C: With her, you are determining the things you want to remember in the coming life?

J: You have decided that you want to go in certain directions to experience and learn certain things. If you go in a different direction, you are not going to learn what you wanted or you are going to put off learning it. You want to stay as close to your map as you can. It is kind of like taking a crayon and making arrows along the way. But the map involves mostly people and things about them. Maybe something they say that catches your attention, or something they do, or how they look.

Studying the Life Map and Embedded Clues

C: Who decides what you are going to notice?

J: You do! And you really study it, because you know it's going to be hard to remember it once you are back in the physical body. A lot of times I don't think you remember consciously, but just enough so you go in the right direction. It's very intense.

C: What are you doing there now?

J: Just continuing to look. As I watch the movie, the teacher brings my attention to the crossroads with her pointer. She points out another place where I can go right or left or backwards or forwards. I need to establish my arrow so I know which direction I will need to go. I go through and establish these directions. Then I review them several times.

I come back two, three, four, as many times as I need, because it's really important. I am getting really close to going back into a human lifetime and I must really try to concentrate and take as much information with me as I can. I want to accomplish everything that I set out to accomplish, to learn, and to do. In between these sessions, I take breaks and relax with my friends, because we are all concentrating so hard. Also, I go to other classes.

Between-life Classes

C: What are these other classes?

J: Spiritual classes. I am learning more about love and how to balance and express the laws of Spirit when I return to the physical.

C: Describe one of those classes?

J: The teacher is explaining responsibility.

C: How many are in the class?

J: Oh golly, about 12, 13, 14.

C: How does the teacher appear?

J: All the students attending this class have agreed how we want its setting to be. The teacher is a young female and she appears as a light blue color. I have an awareness that there is a lot of love there, unless you want to assign a form, she doesn't necessarily show herself in a form. She is pretty much in her light body.

It is interesting, because since I am going to go back into a physical body, physical images are interspersed with the spiritual body. I will be returning to a lifetime where I will deal with the physical and those types of images. Often I will see my guide, the council, or my friends in their soul bodies, and I know who they are, because each one has their own essence.

C: The soul body, as described by Joan, is the body of the true spiritual self.

J: She has like a blackboard, but instead of words, I actually see situations or examples. She is giving a lecture about what responsibility means and how important it is that we are responsible for our thoughts, words, and actions. Because they are all going to have consequences. Whether or not we envision the consequences, we are still responsible. Part of that responsibility is to help other people be responsible for themselves.

C: Are you aware of yourself on a particular level?

J: It's not totally mental, as it seems to be above that, because the communication is through just knowing. You can assign mental images, but you don't have to, because there is a real comfort with just the knowing without the images. That is how most of the communication is done. There is not real physical form to anything.

C: Is there any particular color or hue that characterizes where you are?

J: Varying degrees of blue and a kind of purplish blue.

C: Does this color represent any state of consciousness or advancement?

J: The higher the spiritual consciousness, the brighter and more intense the color is. It might be darker, but it is like an electric blue. It's real bright. The colors seem less solid, even to where sometimes they blink. As I see my friends, we are a little bit more solid. We are light in color but not as bright, and there is not as much flicker, I guess. As a matter of fact, that is one of the ways we can tell who the counselors and guides are, because they have this wonderful flickering. It's like pulsating energy.

C: What else do you do in the class?

J: I go to several classes a day. Each one focuses on something a little different.

C: What are some of the different topics besides responsibility?

J: Love. What real unconditional love is. Discipline, balance, and truth.

C: Do different teachers teach these classes?

J: Yes, each teacher has a specialty.

C: Are the classes taught in different locations?

J: Yes, it is almost like a big, loosely structured building. But you move by shifting your awareness. You don't really have to move, per se.

C: Is there a night where you are?

J: No, and no one gets tired. The activity is interspersed with times of relaxation, but there is no night. There is no day, really. I tend to associate in physical terms with the fact that it's light. I am really busy the whole time. Even when I relax, I just change my focus.

First Parent, Then Child

C: What does Yoseph do with you next?

J: He is pretty involved with forming the physical body of my mother to be at this point.

C: Can you still meet with him while he is involved with your mother?

J: Yes, I do, because I spend time around the mother once the baby's body that I am going to go into is growing.

Like a well-rehearsed play, the entrance of certain souls into a physical life drama is timed to occur at certain key points in what we know as time.

C: Do you spend time with your mother while she is pregnant?

J: Yes.

C: And it is Yoseph who has taken on that body?

J: Yes, at that point, there is recognition. There is a part of him I can communicate with.

C: What is the last activity that you do before you incarnate again?

J: Kind of a review of the roadmap on my own. To try to keep it in memory as much as I can. I am by myself, and it is very quiet. With the help of the teacher, I have marked the certain points. So I just kind of run the film and take note of the various points, looks, locations, smells, etc. I want to try to hold onto that knowledge with the soul as strongly as I can. I think, "Oh, this is going to be easy. I can do this." I forget about what will happen to these memories after I get into the physical body.

C: What do you do after this final review process?

J: Once the baby's body is being prepared in the physical, it's growing within the mother. I want to spend more and more time around her because I want to get tuned in. This is done so that I can just slip in real easily when the time comes. I spend a lot of time around her.

C: When do you slip in?

J: To stay? Just a little bit before the actual birth. Compared to the freedom of being just soul, the body is very constrictive and heavy. So I do not want to spend a lot of time there until I absolutely have to. I know that I need to be around, because there is a certain interfacing that has to take place. This is so you can attune the soul to the body and the body to the soul.

C: How long before the birth do you actually stay in the body?

J: It actually varies, but in this case, about a month beforehand. [She laughs.] I got impatient. Didn't like it and ended up accelerating the whole process so that I was born earlier than they thought I would be. Maybe I chose the point I did because I knew that physically, birth was going to occur before full term. It is like the difference between day and night coming from the freedom of soul into the body of a child who is not yet born.

it isn't the same for everybody

As you can see, there are many considerations that go into the choice of your current lifetime. Not all souls have the awareness and flexibility of choice demonstrated in Joan's example. There are times, for other souls, when the choices involving a future incarnation are largely made for them by the council and guide or guides assigned to the soul. There, as here in this world, we are all at different stages of spiritual awareness, resulting in greater degrees of freedom and opportunity. When a soul, such as Joan, chooses a deeper understanding of love as a primary reason for incarnating, many spiritual hurdles have already been overcome, and that soul has a greater freedom to make key choices for the next life.

a mid-life review

Hopefully you now have some idea what souls go through in preparation for a new incarnation. As you can see, the between-life state can be a very active period of learning and preparation for souls in this universal school of life.

You need not wait until you are between lifetimes to take advantage of some of the jewels of awareness hidden within yourself. If you have the interest and desire, you can access these jewels now and begin to transform your life to a state of greater joy and fulfillment.

With a mid-life review you have an opportunity to make a quantum leap in your karmic awareness and in understanding the relationships that engage you.

To conduct a mid-life review, answer the following questions:

- Consider the significant relationships you've had up till now. They can be romantic relationships, work relationships, friendships, family relationships, etc. What has been the dominant theme of each? Some examples could be acceptance, non-judgment, discipline, accountability, trust, forgiveness, betrayal, honesty, tenacity, and so on. What have you learned about yourself by recognizing and experiencing this relationship theme?

- What have you learned spiritually from the Karmic Relationships you've had in life up until now? What would you do differently in the future to bring them into a place of more unconditional love, balance, and harmony? Are there any Karmic Relationships you could balance out right now?

- Are there certain spiritual classes, courses of study, spiritual guides or masters that might help you learn how to decrease the karma in your Karmic Relationships?

- Why have you made the choices of parents, friends, business associates, classmates, and acquaintances? What spiritual gifts or challenges have they presented to you?

- What were the key transforming experiences
  in your life? The pivotal points or crossroads
  when you felt clear inner guidance?

- What embedded cues can you recall that
  assured you that you were meeting people you
  were supposed to meet and doing what you
  were meant to do? How did you recognize
  them then? How might you identify them in
  the future?

In Chapter 13, we will explore the use of dreams to heal
Karmic Relationships and the different ways dreams can
manifest in your waking self. You'll also be given exercises
to enhance dream recall and get answers to questions about
your life, health, and relationships.

Using Dreams to Repair Karmic Relationships

THE SUBJECT OF DREAMS AND KARMIC RELATIONSHIPS COULD FILL THE pages of this entire book. For many of us dreams are the only doorway we have into the deeper realms of the unconscious and the many levels of heaven. Over the years, I've seen so many past-life dreams that I've often wondered why they've escaped the notice of many great psychotherapist and founders of the well-known schools of psychoanalysis such as Freud, Adler, or Jung. I suspect Jung observed past-life dreams and experiences but never took an official position on them. I can understand why, because even in psychology today we are still wedded to specific dogmas involving the psyche.

When they thrust themselves into conscious awareness, past-life dreams and the relationships they embody are so literal, vivid, and detailed there is no other obvious explanation for them other than that they are actual memories of long ago times and experiences. Because of this, such dreams are seldom, if ever, forgotten.

I've found there is an interactive aspect to the interest many have in certain historical periods or subjects and their own past lives. For example, an interest in history can awaken the unconscious memory of dormant past lives, bringing them closer to conscious awareness. Conversely your unconscious past-life memories may draw your interest to certain subjects or historical periods. Some people have a preoccupation with the Civil War to the extent that they are a part of groups that reenact battle scenes from this era. Others have a fascination and interest in ancient Egyptian culture with a strong desire to study and learn more about it. Such interests are not random or coincidental.

I have a similar love and familiarity with Asian culture, primarily China and Japan. Not too long ago I had a very vivid dream of a past life in Japan. In it, I found myself in the back yard of a traditional Japanese home as a Japanese male with my wife. We were dressed in traditional kimono and sandals. It was a warm summer day with cherry blossoms blooming among the trees. I could feel the warmth of the air and even smell the sweet aromas in the breeze. We stood in front of a garden pond full of koi (Japanese carp), experiencing the feelings of serenity, joy, and contentment often associated with traditional Asian homes and gardens. This dream experience was free of symbolic distortions or anything out of the ordinary that is characteristic of more common dreams. It simply was as if I were literally there. When I awoke, I had the immediate realization that this had been me in a past life.

This dream and many other experiences and realizations clearly explain why I've had a love for Asian culture and aesthetics. Over the years, I've had several dream experiences reflecting past-life ties to Japan, China, and many other cultures.

Conversely, Billy Bob Thornton, the well-known actor and director, has an irrational fear of Asian antiques. From a radio interview heard on National Public Radio (NPR), it's my understanding it is a near phobic reaction in which he can't bear to be around such furniture. He has no known explanation for this in his current life experience. I suspect that like Benito, my young Brazilian client, Billy Bob carries an unconscious trauma associated with an Asian past life.

Such unconscious past-life memories are why certain places and historical periods may seem familiar to you as you travel the world. It could be ancient Japan or China like myself, or the Victorian era, the Middle Ages, Ancient Rome, Egypt, and so on.

past-life traumatic dreams

In my case there was no trauma involved in my past-life dream, but many do have dream recall of traumatic past lives. Such dreams have great therapeutic value when understood correctly.

In my tape/CD set, *The Way of Karma*, I tell the story of Dr. Nelson, a 35-year-old Jewish physician with a thriving practice. He had what is best described as a past-life dream the night prior to his first appointment with me. He recalled a dream in which he saw himself as an old black male slave who was put into the cotton fields with the women. He had to fill his weight criteria of cotton daily or be beaten. He also described having a right hip problem. This was all he could recall of the dream.

Dr. Nelson came to me because he had a fear of authority, specifically male authority. Because there were no incidents in his life that would account for his fears, they seemed quite irrational to him. As a physician, he was able to suppress his fears, but they were a constant source of stress and resulted in a certain awkwardness at times. This was especially the case when he had to treat males he perceived as having positions of authority themselves. He had tried traditional psychotherapy, relaxation, and even medication. Finally, unable to think of anywhere else to turn, he came to see me.

As you might have guessed by now from his dream, it became the catalyst for our first Soul Journeys session taking Dr. Nelson into a past life when he was a black male slave in America. We followed that lifetime from the time he was captured by slave traders in Africa, shackled below the ship's deck, shipped across the seas to America, and finally sold at port to a plantation owner.

In that life he picked cotton in the fields. As expected, during that time, he suffered great abuse and at one point had his right leg and hip broken by white teenage boys who assaulted him for sport. He recovered from the injury, but years later died in a barn of another brutal beating at the hands of young whites.

The upside to this story was that during his convalescence from the broken leg and hip, a very compassionate white physician treated his injuries. During this time he was allowed to heal and recover in a bed where black women house slaves took care of him. The doctor had left such a favorable impression on him, that it instilled a desire in this soul to become a healer; one which he fulfilled in this lifetime by becoming a physician.

Considering the death he remembered in that life, it was no wonder Dr. Nelson feared authority, even though he is white in this lifetime and a physician with authority to others. Dr. Nelson also noted that he'd always felt a curious affinity for African-Americans.

freedom from past-life baggage

It is said by some that you never really get rid of your baggage; you just learn how to carry it better. This may be true with traditional psychotherapy. However, with Soul Journeys I've come to expect my clients to eventually be completely free of the baggage we target during our sessions together. As stated earlier in the book, this occurs rather quickly, as a paradigm shift, after a series of sessions.

My experience with Dr. Nelson was no exception. After our sessions he found himself free of the fear of authority that had plagued him throughout his adult life. Like the many who resolve past-life trauma in this manner, the transition from fear to resolution was quite natural. It's like something foreign has been removed, allowing you freedom to just be yourself. Finally Dr. Nelson was able to live and practice without the unconscious irrational fear that authority figures posed an unidentified danger.

from cloudy to clearer dream recall

When we first begin the therapy process, often many dreams aren't recalled. But as we progress, the door then opens to greater recall and acceptance of dream messages from the unconscious. Heather fell into the category of someone who moved into clearer and more helpful dreams.

After the second of a series of three sessions I had with her, Heather had a past-life dream that pointed to her fear of abandonment and over-attachment to her current family. Typical of past-life dreams it was a clear, vivid, but brief episode.

In the dream she found herself as a little girl of around 12-years-old with sandy blonde hair. This was World War II, and she was a Holocaust victim. She was standing in the crowded cattle car of a train. The bodies were so tightly packed she could barely breath. She struggled to remain standing as someone tripped and fell against her. In the dream, Heather was aware that her best friend today had been in the cattle car with her in that lifetime.

Occurring four nights prior to our third and final session, this dream was a way for Heather's inner self to alert me that past-life trauma needed to be resolved. During our next session Heather experienced being taken away from her home, separated from her mother and brother, and put into the back of a crowded, tarp-covered truck.

In Heather's words: "Everybody was crying and screaming. Suddenly a Nazi soldier hit a woman on the side of the head with the butt of his rifle."

In that life the child, whom Heather had been, sat quietly in the corner, noticing blood dripping from the battered woman's head. The little girl never saw her family again and was gassed to death in the camp.

This past life was one of several I took Heather through to resolve abandonment fears and separation anxiety. Her prior dream served as a diagnostic that led us directly into her past life during the Holocaust.

Over the years I've guided many clients through the Holocaust in past lives. One African American woman comes to mind; she was a German Jew in her past life, separated from her family in the death camps, and later gassed to death. I mention this because during this session she spontaneously lapsed into speaking fluent German while describing the trauma. In her present life awareness she had no knowledge of the German language.

On occasion during Soul Journey sessions, this happens and I've observed clients speaking French, German, Latin, Native American tongues, and other more obscure languages they have no knowledge of in their daily life awareness. During the Soul Journey session they are easily able to translate what they are saying into English, but it's often easier for them to say it first in the language they originally experienced the trauma in.

past-life dreams are designed to be remembered

Often past-life dreams involving trauma will leave the dreamer shaken or disturbed upon awakening. Yet they are difficult to forget because of their clarity.

Dreams, under the direction of the soul or the higher self, seem to adapt to fit the language and understanding of the dreamer. For this reason the unconscious mind will generally cooperate with our assumptions about life, limited as they may be, and censor or distort that which is unacceptable to us.

This principle also appears to extend to the psycho-therapist you may see to resolve some unwanted block, pattern, or fear. Your unconscious will naturally limit or expand itself by expressing dreams that approximate the framework and beliefs of the therapist.

Clients of a Freudian therapist will have dreams that symbolically suggest sexual motivations and impulses that are congruent with Freudian psychology.

Jungian therapists' clients will have dreams that fit a Jungian model. Sometime it's also just a matter of inter-pretation. The same dream can be interpreted in different ways depending on the therapist. Because my first therapeutic orien-tation was primarily Jungian, I observed this phenomena with my own clients and with those of colleagues who had different therapeutic orientations.

Then there are the past-life dreams. These dreams are unmistakable by their literalness and lucidity. The appearance of past-life dreams is not necessarily a response to the therapist's orientation. At times, clients would recount what were vivid and traumatic past-life dreams they experienced months or many years before ever seeing a therapist. With these very literal and memorable dreams, any other interpretation would be a stretch.

Realizing there could be a potential conflict with a therapist's orientation, clients, who didn't necessarily believe in past lives, wouldn't know how to view such dreams so they would just report them. I've even received referrals from other therapist's when people they were seeing reported such vivid unexplained dreams. It was as if their unconscious knew there would be a time when this information would be valuable for their healing.

The inner self somehow knows the understanding and limits of the therapist. For this reason some, who have never had anything approximating past-life dreams, will often begin having them just prior to or during therapy. This makes the direction of our work together much clearer. It's almost as if they become willing participants and observers in the communication between their inner self and myself as therapist.

My acceptance and understanding of the spiritual as well as emotional and psychological modalities includes the allowance for past lives as credible therapy material. This acceptance allows the unconscious through dreams to present literal, undistorted material from past lifetimes thereby offering the most direct route for healing. Letting past-life dreams be just what they are—memories of actual events—cuts directly through the sometimes confusing and misleading symbolic/literal dream mixes or the purely symbolic dream interpretations with which most of us are familiar.

The unconscious cooperates with the healing process by providing dreams that most directly relate to one's needs for healing and understanding their Karmic Relationships.

therapeutic past-life dreams

As with Dr. Nelson, my clients often have past-life dreams the night before their first appointment with me or sometime during the course of therapy. Certainly this is not necessary, but it happens often enough.

Because of this pattern, I inquire about dreams during my initial intake interviews. I also suggest that a person watch their dreams more closely during the time period when we're having our sessions together. These dreams can be very instructive and act as signposts to direct the therapy. On many occasions, clients have had dreams of traumatic past lives that have had the greatest impact on their present-life. They have even had dreams that gave insight into the progression of the therapy. Grace's story below is a good example of how therapeutic dreams can help to guide healing.

From the time she was five years old, Grace had had a recurring dream of being in the basement of a house that was filled with dirty water. She'd see herself swimming to stay alive. There was just enough space between the water level and the basement ceiling to keep her head above the water and allow her to breathe. This dream had repeatedly frightened Grace, leaving her anxious and upset.

Grace is a middle-aged computer programmer for a utility company. Her childhood was full of challenge that included some of the worst sexual abuse I had ever been told about. The abuse had resulted in Grace's own sexual dysfunction and alcoholism. The early loss of both alcoholic parents didn't make life any easier for her. She had numerous fears and phobias such as claustrophobia, a fear of being homeless, and fear of being falsely arrested. She also had chronic pain in various parts of her body.

I saw Grace weekly for approximately three months. During the course of that time we went through and resolved many very traumatic past lives that had impact on the childhood sexual abuse of this lifetime. In most of Grace's past lives, she had been the victim of some sort of abuse.

the karmic root of grace's victim experiences

Even though there were several lives when Grace recalled being a woman who was victimized, the series of Grace's past-life Soul Journeys finally culminated with a different type of past-life experience. In this life, which preceded the others when she'd been a victim, she had been a man in England.

This man was a wealthy but cruel landowner with a huge estate and many enemies. In that life Grace described herself as a feudal, mean character that wore draped clothes and a jacket trimmed with velvet or fur. Even though he wore pants with stockings, he was not foppish. His medium-brown hair was long and curly. He lived in a big stone house with many servants. There, he drank and brooded a lot.

The man was married but he felt unhappy, isolated, and alone. He tortured and abused the people who worked for him throughout his estate and the surrounding lands. On occasion, he would ride through the community on horse-back, carrying a whip and flanked by two guards. He was a feared tyrant who had his enemies killed. He even tortured and abused his wife. Finally she betrayed him with another man and became pregnant. When he found out, he badly burned her between the legs with a hot poker and threw her out, leaving her destitute and seriously wounded. She had to starve or live off the land with the peasants.

His wife never recovered from her injuries and fell ill. She was being cared for by what he called a witch woman or local healer.

He had heard from his handlers of his wife's severe illness, so he went to the hut to see her just before she died. Watching her burning with fever, he was suddenly stricken with grief and sorrow at what he had done. He pleaded and begged her forgiveness and was angry with himself and even with God. That night, he rode home with his handlers and drank till he passed out.

After his wife's death his drinking and his depression got much worse. He went to the local priest, who was also afraid of him, and confessed the awful things he'd done. It didn't help. He hated himself and continued to seek relief in the wine bottle.

Sometimes at night, he would go out drunk to visit his wife's grave and talk to her. By Grace's accounts, he was a very good horseman, but on one of these nights, while riding drunk, he hit a tree branch. It flung him off his horse and threw him to the ground, paralyzing him from the neck down.

There was nothing the doctors could do for him but try to keep him sedated with drugs and alcohol. His condition grew steadily worse. As he lay on his deathbed, he began thinking: "I wish I could have done things differently. I didn't need to be so mean. I'm so tired. I want to start over and have a chance to be a boy again. I know I will go to hell. I don't care. My wife was so wonderful, and I killed her."

He had three children, two boys and a girl, who were brought into the room. He told them not to be like him because he was a wicked man.

He then saw his deceased mother, father, and brother in the room there to welcome him across the threshold of death. According to Grace, they looked so loving and held their hands out to him. His deceased wife also appeared and told him she forgave him. He was unable to look at her because of his shame and guilt. He also saw his three children who had died. Grace said that they all looked to the dying man to be so happy and beautiful.

As Grace relived her death in this past life, she said that the man could clearly see his deceased family members in front of him. They all were calling for him to come to them. He thought, "I don't deserve that. I'm too wicked."

He surveyed the room and took it all in—his deceased parents, brother, wife, and children as well as his living sister, her husband, and his three children. He even noticed the servant in the corner tending to the fire. Finally taking his last breath, he left the body.

the courage to face the past

This series of past lives, which Grace experienced in our sessions, were particularly traumatic, and I admired her courage to face them. Her childhood sexual abuse, the alcoholism, and the other fears and pain she carried required that we resolve these lives to bring about healing. The last life she experienced as a wealthy but abusive landowner was actually the root cause of her lives as a victim and had precipitated her current lifetime experiences.

Unfortunately, not many people are ready or willing to face and resolve this type of past-life trauma. It is for this reason that I believe there is resistance by some to accept the notion of past lives. Such acceptance would result in needing to take responsibility for all of our thoughts, words, and actions. How many of us are really ready for that?

For this reason religious bias against belief in reincarnation, in some cases, can be a convenient rationalization in service of the ego. I've found we all carry baggage from past lives into this one. I have also found that directly facing past-life material is a requirement to completely freeing yourself of invisible wounds.

We face ourselves either slowly over numerous lifetimes or more rapidly through specialized intervention such as Soul Journeys therapy or focused spiritual practice. Even though it's comparatively brief, this process can be very intense. The adage: "No pain, no gain," certainly applies with cases like Grace's.

With little success Grace had read many self-help books and had done traditional therapies for years. This is quite understandable considering her unresolved past-life trauma. In addition to her presenting complaints, her self-worth and self-esteem had also remained low because of guilt and shame stemming from unconscious past and present-life influences.

After our series of sessions, for the first time in her life Grace began to feel free of the discomfort and pain in her body. Even though her job was stressful, she now experienced a lightness and joy that hadn't been there before. Her sexual desire started to return and finally Grace was able to see light at the end of the tunnel.

a wrap-up and confirmation dream

Toward the end of our sessions, Grace had her basement dream again. This time, instead of finding herself up to her neck in the dingy water, she was asking her younger brother to go down into the basement and check on the situation. In this dream Grace herself went into the basement after work (therapy) and saw that it was no longer filled with water. The floor was still quite dirty with cigarette butts lying around, but she saw only a little puddle of water off to one side.

In Grace's case, the water in her dream symbolized the emotional pain and trauma of her unconscious (the basement), which had accumulated from her past lives. Since childhood, this water had threatened to drown her and left little room for her to breath (survive). Finally, the water had been largely drained away with only cleanup work left to do in the basement (cigarette butts and dirt). Her brother symbolized the male polarity she needed to face in her past lives so she could heal her invisible wounds.

breaking through mental barriers

Dreams are instructive, informative, healing, and enlightening. One question I ask right away is if someone has had recurrent dreams or nightmares. Even though such dreams can rattle the conscious mind, they surface with a strong emotional charge to point out some important issue or information. There is a valuable message contained in such dreams. Often these dreams offer fragments of past-life trauma either literally presented by the unconscious or censored and disguised symbolically to accommodate a lack of acceptance of reincarnation. As stated earlier, I've even seen literal past-life dreams break through for someone who did not believe in reincarnation at all. In these instances the soul is trying to achieve emotional balance within the psyche and break through the limitations of cultural or religious beliefs.

Simply because you're reading this book, you are likely to begin having dreams pointing to or previewing your own past lives. If you invite such dreams, Spirit is even more likely to bring them directly into your conscious awareness. As with my dream of a Japanese past life, past-life dreams need not necessarily involve trauma. You've lived many past lives in which you have been joyful and pain-filled, rich and poor, powerful and weak, healthy and sickly, caring and ruthless.

When you reach a point such as now, where you seek a greater understanding of the purpose behind the drama of life, it may be time for you to take even greater responsibility for your destiny as soul.

Using the Past-Life Museum exercise in Chapter 11 will open the door wider for you to experience your own past lives, invisible wounds, and Karmic Relationships.

Dreams are just another avenue to open pathways for you, as soul, to glimpse and experience more of the divine drama. There you can meet souls you've known for ages or with whom you've had significant past-life exchanges. This may include an array of Karmic Relationships such as love partners, parents, friends, and associates.

afterlife and other-world dreams

Just as you may have distorted past-life dreams full of symbols and disguised meaning to protect your disbelieving conscious mind, your "common" dreams also may have some unwelcome distortions and symbolic disguises.

Your dreams include many souls you have known in your current life and also those who have passed on to the other side. These earthly and afterlife relationships are also part of the divine drama I spoke of earlier.

Once you expand your parameters of belief and acceptance, you may have conscious, vivid, and very literal dreams of the many levels of heaven. The soul within will only expose you to what you are ready for and need to face or understand.

I often interact in very literal ways in the dream state with friends, ancestors, love partners, spiritual guides, and *Beings* that are unknown to me in my waking life. These dreams are more like travels into other dimensions than dreams and go way beyond the limits of my day-to-day life. Yet, these encounters and experiences in the dream state have great practical value and integrate directly into my waking daily life and personal growth.

dreams and karmic relationships

The following is an example of one of my own Karmic Relationships and how healing through the dream state helped me to resolve and release my emotions surrounding it.

On one occasion a long-distance relationship I had been in abruptly ended. I had suspected that there were some things she would not or could not tell me. One day, I sat in my apartment near the beach and felt the need for a heart-to-heart discussion with my girlfriend who was visiting me at the time. She was due to fly back home within a day or two. Sensing my concern, she held my hand, looked into my eyes, and asked me to trust her—that all was just fine between us. She promised that she would return within a month.

She flew back home a couple days later. In the following days after her departure, I called and we spoke on the phone in only brief conversations. She sounded extremely agitated. She admitted that she was unraveling emotionally and would need a little time to sort things out. Sensing again that she was holding something back, I asked if she still wanted to maintain our commitment as a couple. I knew it would be painful to break up with her now, but wanted to face the truth if this was the beginning of the end of our relationship.

She assured me that she would call soon to explain. She never did call, and out of respect for her request to allow her to call me when ready, I didn't initiate another call to her even though there was a great desire to. I haven't seen her since—at least, physically.

As you can imagine I had many unanswered questions and unresolved feelings about this breakup. After about six months, I had a series of dreams for seven consecutive nights. Each night in the dream state, my former girlfriend and I were seated in a room where we faced each other. These dreams were as real and lucid as if we sat somewhere in a physical room.

During the dreams we had the opportunity to discuss our relationship and all that had occurred. I asked her many questions. At times, she gave honest answers; at other times, she was evasive. Curiously, in this state even when she was evasive, I clearly saw the truth of her thoughts and feelings. Nothing could be hidden. Because of this transparency of perception, I eventually was able to understand more than she could tell me in person. This enabled me to have compassion for her and accept that she had done the best she could.

I knew from our previous conversations that she came from a family where both her parents were alcoholic and had been physically and emotionally abusive to her. She had been in a marriage in which her husband was said to abuse drugs and even her at times. Her wounds ran deep. In spite of her best efforts, it seemed her history made the prospect of our relationship too much of a challenge.

When we were together, I had felt the tension in her body just under the surface and wondered if she ever truly relaxed. From these dreams I learned that she had reached her limit of love and intimacy in our relationship and hit a wall she could not or would not pass through. After the series of dream discussions, I was able to get closure and finally put the relationship to rest. For me, none of the emotional residue remained of what we had together, save understanding and some sadness.

Because there had been no opportunity to have these conversations with her in person physically, I was allowed, as soul, to resolve my feelings and heal emotional pain in the dream worlds. However, this could not have happened if not for my openness to the fact that it's possible to have conscious meetings and exchanges in the dream state.

other functions of dream and karmic healing

The example above of my Karmic Relationship shows only one of the infinite opportunities for healing hidden karmic wounds using dreams. Other ways dreams can help you heal include offering you health advice or warnings, financial insights, and answering your questions. You can even take classes in the dream state to further your knowledge and understanding. It's obvious that to take full advantage of the opportunities available through dreams you have to learn to recall your experiences or be conscious during them, even while your body sleeps.

There are several ways to develop or sharpen dream recall. I've outlined below some I've found useful over the years.

Preparations/Strategies to Enhance Dream Recall

- Keep a nightly dream journal.

- Eat your last meal in the early evening. Try not to sleep on a full stomach.

- Avoid the use of alcoholic beverages on nights you wish vivid dream recall.

- Take special notice of outstanding or unusual details or events during the day.

- Get to bed early enough to feel rested.

- Take daytime naps. Often dream recall is easier during these times.

- Upon first awakening, lie still to reflect on various dreams you may have had.

- Meditate or say a brief prayer prior to bed.

- Wake yourself at 3 or 4 A.M., get up, and reflect on or journal any dreams you may have had. Reaffirm your intent to recall dreams and go back to sleep until you would normally awaken.

- Use the experience of falling in dreams as a cue to relax, become lucid, and fly. Decide to do this before going to sleep at night.

- Never leave a disturbing dream unresolved. Lie in bed or sit quietly with your eyes closed and seek a favorable resolution through the use of your creative imagination.

dream recall exercises

In addition to the techniques above, there are two more methods for working with dreams that I've found to be especially important and effective.

The first I call "The Dream Question." This exercise involves taking any question you have about your life, health, relationships, or whatever, and write it down briefly and clearly on a piece of paper. Before you retire at night read aloud this question with the request that you be given a clear, unambiguous answer in the dream state. Place the paper under your pillow and sleep on it.

It may take several nights before your answer comes, but be patient. Your answer may also come through some event or message in your waking life; better known as the "waking dream." Either way, if you are sincere, an answer will come.

The second technique is designed to enhance dream recall tenfold. It is for those who don't remember their dreams at all or who want to make dream recall even sharper than the usual ability to recall daily life experiences. I call this "The Reverse Chronology Exercise." I've also found this exercise an excellent preparation for those with serious doubts about their ability to experience past lives. If practiced daily for a week or more prior to Soul Journeys sessions recall is significantly enhanced.

Near the end of the evening, find a quiet place and review your day in reverse chronology, or backwards. This means you are to recall the thing you just did before you sat to do this exercise, the thing before that, and so on until you have reviewed your entire day, ending with when you first got up in the morning. You should take no longer than 15 to 20 minutes for this exercise. Throughout your review notice certain thoughts and feelings associated with events. Especially take note of anything unusual or out of the ordinary.

Do this review nightly as a discipline. The results will be obvious when you awaken in the morning to review your dreams. You'll find that your recall has increased greatly. This exercise has the added benefit of strengthening your conscious awareness of all that you experience, whether waking or sleeping.

The Reverse Chronology exercise addresses the fact that maybe 95 percent of the time we are actually living life unconsciously or asleep even during our so-called waking hours. Preoccupied with the past or anticipating the future, we do not live in the ever present *Now*, as Eckhart Tolle has so elegantly written about in his book, *The Power of Now: A Guide to Spiritual Enlightenment*. Our actions and reactions are largely mechanical in nature. Combine these with conditioned responses from past-life trauma, and there is little chance for conscious action.

Your waking life and Karmic Relationships are much like your dreams. They unconsciously roll from one event to the next if you don't examine their direction or stop to gain perspective on how they fit into your life and its purpose.

a reflection on purpose

The heart and purpose behind this entire book is to make you more aware of the freedom and potential in your present-life by freeing you from negative influences and wounds stemming from past-lives or pre-birth experiences. With this freedom you will grow to view death as merely a transition into a familiar place called home and rebirth as a natural occurrence.

When you've gained freedom from fear and negativity, you can more easily take full and conscious responsibility for all you do or that comes into your life. You will have no need to project blame or accept a victim mentality. With this new awareness, you can heal your hidden wounds and release the karma and emotions that are keeping your Karmic Relationships in destructive cycles.

Your next step is to transcend karma completely and live by the law of love. Life then becomes a creative dance, inspired by the ideas, projects, and people you love. Everything you do, no matter how small or seemingly insignificant, will become an expression of that love. You will be a shining light here and everywhere, including in the dream worlds.

epilogue

As you might imagine, this book has been years in the making. When I first started doing Soul Journeys sessions back in the early 1980s, there was little knowledge of such work, and it was considered very esoteric. Yet I often wondered what the world would think if they could but witness or experience the many wondrous transformations I saw in my work. Even today, the experiences of the Soul Journeying through time never ceases to amaze and sometimes challenge me.

In the face of all this, it is important for me to stay out of the way while facilitating the process each individual goes through in the journey to wholeness and deep spiritual understanding. It is my gift to witness such transformations. I've written this book to share that gift of transformation with you in hopes that you may glimpse the possibilities for your own healing and enlightenment.

Certainly traditional therapy has its place, but psychology in its highest expression is the science of the soul. This essence has gotten lost in the preoccupation with the ego, mind, and emotions. It's now time to resurrect the soul in psychology. For the soul is our only true and permanent identity. When psychotherapy denies or ignores this truth, it is like elevating the status of a car over its driver, the plane over its passengers.

It's important for all to realize that the soul can fly free to explore greater realms at will. There is no need for it to remain limited like a bird in a cage.

A story among the Blackfoot Indians comes to mind of an Indian brave who climbed a steep cliff and came across an untended eagle's nest. Removing one of the eggs, he brought it to his village and placed it in a hen's nest to hatch. Born into the world was a little eaglet that thought it was a chicken. Following the example of the mother hen, the young eagle learned to walk and held its head lowered to the ground. The eaglet scratched in the dirt, pecking at worms and seeds.

One day, when he was fully grown, the eagle looked up and saw a magnificent bird soaring across the heavens.

"What is that?" he asked his family.

"That's an eagle," answered the old grandma hen. She knew many things about the world or at least she thought she did.

"How wonderful it must be to fly so high," he said.

"Yes, it must be," she agreed. "But forget it. You're just a chicken."

So without further question, the eagle lived out the rest of his life with the limits of a chicken, scratching in the dirt.

As soul, for many lifetimes we have lived lives unaware of our true birthright. The door is always open if we would just explore beyond the boundaries of our long held assumptions.

This can only be done in a spirit of love. Yes, there is karma, but it serves only to teach us the lessons of power.

As soul, we all share that same journey to fully realize the Godhood within. We teach each other the greater lessons of love. This is the mystery and the promise behind Karmic Relationships.

about charles l. richards, ph.d.

CHARLES L. RICHARDS, PH.D., a psychotherapist licensed in marriage, family, and child counseling, is in private practice in San Diego, California. He specializes in Soul Journeys therapy and Karmic Analysis. These processes, which he developed, allow people to recall and heal the invisible emotional wounds of past-life, pre-birth, birthing, and between-life traumas that are affecting their current relationships.

Healthcare professionals and therapists regularly refer their patients to Dr. Richards and invite him to speak and train them on his work and methodology. National television recognition for Dr. Richards's work came about through his appearances on *The Other Side* and an NBC television special. He's been interviewed on radio and television news shows and has been the subject of numerous newspaper articles in the United States, Brazil, and Australia.

Dr. Richards, who has taught graduate level courses in psychology, received his doctorate in clinical psychology in 1982 from Alliant International University in San Diego. He's been a member of the Association for Past-Life Research and Therapy, and has trained CEOs of Fortune 500 corporations in management and leadership development at the Center for Creative Leadership.

Dr. Richards has used his therapy with over one thousand patients, many of whom have come from the United States, Canada, Europe, South America, and Australia. He has presented his lectures, classes, and workshops worldwide including the Chopra Center for Well Being in San Diego, The Learning Annex, The University for Humanistic Studies, and The Association for Black Psychologists.

Dr. Richards established the Soul Journeys Institute to offer therapy, workshops, referrals, and train other therapists in Soul Journeys therapy and Karmic Analysis.

For additional information, please visit his Website at
www.karmicrelationships.com.

Or you can write or call direct at:

DHARMATEK
P.O. Box 4275
Leucadia, CA 92023
(760) 633-2919
e-mail: DrChasZ@aol.com

We hope this JODERE GROUP book has benefited you
in your quest for personal, intellectual,
and spiritual growth.

JODERE GROUP is passionate about bringing new
and exciting books such as *Karmic Relationships*
to readers worldwide. Our company was created as a
unique publishing and multimedia avenue for individuals
whose mission it is to positively impact the lives of others.
We recognize the strength of an original thought, a kind
word and a selfless act—and the power of the
individuals who possess them. We are committed
to providing the support, passion, and creativity
necessary for these individuals to achieve
their goals and dreams.

JODERE GROUP is comprised of a dedicated and creative
group of people who strive to provide the highest quality
of books, audio programs, online services, and live
events to people who pursue life-long learning.
It is our personal and professional commitment
to embrace our authors, speakers, and readers
with helpfulness, respect, and enthusiasm.

For more information about
our products, authors, or live events,
please call (800) 569-1002
or visit us on the Web at
www.jodere.com

JODERE
GROUP